Using the NAI[1]

A Work in Progress

PAUL SPENCER BYARD

Essay 01

ARCHITECTURE BULLETIN N° 01|2006

Libraries are places of ultimate repose for books and drawings. For them the hard work is done. Their drawn or built or written arguments have been worked out, found readable and then acknowledged by some standard as being worth trying to save and keep available. The standard maybe catholic and generous: on all the shelves and drawers of the globe, no book or drawing is exactly alone. But they have all arrived in what is for each of them a kind of heaven.

Libraries are likewise places of temporary repose for works in progress. These transients land with their authors on libraries like welcome floating branches or pallets. Sometimes when we land on them – as at the NAI – we are relieved to look around at what looks very much like Paradise.

My work in progress – the one that alighted with me at the NAI for two months in the fall of 2005 - is now in draft at W.W. Norton and Company. It's part of more than forty years of practice as an architect and as a lawyer trying to understand what old architecture does for us, not strictly for its usefulness but for what it expresses. What does old architecture do for us by what it says that makes us want to save it? More precisely, what does old

Paul Spencer Byard (1939) is a partner in Platt Byard Dovell White Architects and director of the Historic Preservation Program at the Columbia University Graduate School of Architecture, Planning and Preservation (New York USA). His book, The Architecture of Additions, describes his extensive research on the integration of modern additions into historically significant buildings. As a Guggenheim Fellow, he developed a model in the publication Starting Fresh. Architecture and Historic Preservation in the Twenty-First Century for the theory and practice of American historic buildings policy. He spent considerable time researching that book in the NAI Library and Archives.

architecture do for all of us that allows us to require by law that it be saved?

The question is central to the purpose of historic preservation – why we do it – and to its uniqueness, its extraordinary power. At least in the United States, historic preservation is the first discipline to have the power to enforce architectural expression. What public interest justifies and controls that power in the case of old architecture? And the question, of course, is central to the making of architecture itself. What are we trying to do when we make our buildings say something in the first place? And why do we try so hard? Is what matters what we make them say or is it also something they reveal about us whether we want them to or not?

Perched in the clear light of the NAI reading room, I was asking these questions in order to ground a theory and practice of historic preservation in something more than emotion and politics, to ground it in principle. I had earlier found answers in principle to other basic questions about architecture and historic preservation. My earlier book *The Architecture of Additions: Design and Regulation* (W.W. Norton and Company 1998) surveyed some sixty additions from St.-Peter's in Rome to LeFresnoy outside of Lille to see what in fact happens when you add architecture to architecture and then, more precisely, to suggest what ought to happen when the outcome is controlled in the name of historic preservation. Additions proposed principles for saying what historic preservation is about and how you know when you have done it. The theory and practice would now ideally go on to say in principle why we save old architecture in the first place.

I got to the NAI reading room by the happiest of accidents – and also, of course, in the exercise of supreme good judgment. According to my contract with W.W. Norton, I was due to write on the theory and practice of historical preservation. As Director of the Historic Preservation Program, I was already seven years into the process of trying to reform and give intellectual rigor to the historic preservation curriculum at Columbia University in New York, the birthplace of American historic preservation, and needed the theoretical centerpiece. The cause itself was the cause of a professional lifetime, including work thirty years ago as a lawyer in the Penn Central case that put the force of law in the United States behind historic preservation. The cause was the core of a thirty year design practice as an architect trying not just to do right by old architecture but to make the most of what it can do for us. And the cause was ripe. These are appalling times in the United States. It isn't just in the Bush administration that post-modern "sauve qui peut" conservatism has institutionalized lawless-

fig. 1.1 Library and Aula at TU Delft
photo's: Christian Richters

idem   fig.1.2

ness and abuse. Any architect who prac-tises before local preservation agencies bears the marks and scars of unprincipled populist demagoguery. Carefully assem-bled Modern protective jurisdictions for old architecture are being surrendered by public servants "corrupted" by politics, forced to please whoever shouts loudest. We all write in the end to do what we can to save the world. It was time to pitch in for the sake of principle here.

To get time to write, I put the idea of the work in progress – the public interest in old architecture – to the John Simon Guggenheim Foundation and they liked it, even though I was by their standards rather old. I thought it made sense to go to Rome to write it, but then came the happy accident: the American Academy didn't agree. Close upon the happy acci-dent then came the exercise of supreme good judgment: I thought of Aaron Betsky and the NAI.

Historic preservation as a public cause is, after all, a Modern invention, the last great reform of self-reforming Modernism. It was Modernists like Lucio Costa in Brazil, for example, who saw the continuity of old and new archi-tecture, what they are each expressing for our benefit. It was leftist Modernists like James Marston Fitch in the United States who saw the absurdity of creating false oppositions between old and new by the demolition of one in favor of the other. Where is the continuity of old and new architecture more evident, better observed and made more of than in the Netherlands? What better place to write about old and new architecture as one piece than at the NAI?

I had certain clues that I was right, no-tably, the gratifying, envious gleam that grew in the eyes of Ken Frampton and Mark Wigley as each of them absorbed where I proposed to go. Then there was Aaron Betsky. We had met in a happy if futile effort to get truth and beau-ty to prevail in a big competition in Washington D.C. I knew at his institu-

fig. 1.3   Aula at TU Delft at the end of the 1960s
photo: Fas Keuzenkamp

3

tion I would feel the best spirit and be under the right intellectual aegis.

Architectural libraries are optimistic places, not grim replays of disaster like law libraries, or images of creeping disease like libraries of medicine. Watch people open folios on the white tables of the NAI and see the smiles spread over their faces. Open the Wassmuth Wright the Librarian has spontaneously laid out for you and feel the inherent optimism of Wright's astonishing proposals for what we ought to build to be what we ought to be. The pleasure of it isn't incidental, it's the heart of the matter, the peculiar gift of architecture.

That, at least, is the thesis that began to emerge from the compost of ideas and experience in the mind of the writer at his laptop in the bustling, clattering silence of the NAI reading room. Each work of architecture comes into the world as an argument for itself under the immediate circumstances of its times. Its argument is about improvement, a mixture of ethics and optimism: this is what we need and this is the way to go to get it. Each work of architecture has the last word, but only for minutes, until the next work comes along arguing for itself: no, no, this is the way to go. Together with every other contemporary work they join a garrulous rabble of propositions — like floor traders with their hands up looking for trades — about our times and what we ought to do about them. Crucially they are proposi-

tions we can't avoid. Fixed and enduring right in front of us, right where we want to go, architecture makes us take in its proposals and reflect about our state. How in fact are we doing? Is this the way to go? What should we do about it?

Then architecture ages. Its argument becomes an argument about the past, about what we used to think we needed in order to live as we should. And then comes historic preservation to protect these expressions of the best thinking of the past, the amazing lessons old and new architecture together offer us about our samenesses and our differences, how we should do at least as well as we used to and how we should do better. This history is useful for all of us. Architecture's gift is a gift to humanity, not just to a few cognoscenti. Furthermore, it's not just talk. It's grounded in reality — visitable fixed chunks of built reality that provoke and control what we make of it, that limit our spin.

Thus the thesis that began to emerge on the laptop on my white table as the core of the theory and practice, a view of architecture new and old as precious instructive material for the making of our lives. All around were examples to illustrate it, not the least the NAI itself, in the argument for architecture that got built to Jo Coenen's designs, but also in the other arguments about architecture in the competition models you can still see in the Van Nelle factory.

The best examples were not so much in the library as in the minds of its librarians. Librarians – particularly at the NAI – are welcoming but they are also properly on their guard: each new reader could represent a terrific nuisance. If you are not, though, what librarians give you is a precious kind of intellectual intelligence, a knowledge of the ground that will in the best instances confirm and lead you on beyond what you have in mind yourself – a kind of tipping off: if you look here, you will find that. Alfred Marks was the friend who led me to the greatest riches. Some of it was fun: if you want to go to The Hague, go on Tuesday which happens to be Princesday and you will see not just the Queen but the wonderful shaggy parade that goes with her to the Parliament. And so on a beautiful autumn afternoon, tipped off by Alfred, I could go on my Gazelle to the Panorama of Mesdag, to the Berlage museum and by happy accident to the crest of the very viewpoint of the Panorama, and a memorable sight of the great curve of sunlit North Sea cliffs beyond Scheveningen.

The confirmations were crucial: no, said Alfred, you are not mad to take the Aula at the University of Delft seriously. It could become an example to illustrate the thesis, putting it together with its pendant, the new TU Library. I first read the example backwards, starting with the new Library. Then I realized as I visited it that it made much more sense – indeed only made sense – when read in combination with the Aula. Yes, confirmed TU Dean Beunderman across the hubbub of the opening of the Team 10 Exhibition, that's what Francine Houben of Mecanoo Architects had in mind!

So I got from NAI and the world around it a wonderful example of the way the thesis would have us read old and new architecture together and of the public interest in what we would get from the process. The Aula is an extraordinarily vivid argument about its times, a mighty concrete diplodocus – or Star Wars fighter – poised on the flat bare Modernist ground plane in a state of incipient resistance and extreme watchfulness. Its times were near the peak of the Cold War. The ground-plane now was less an image of the fresh start towards something better – the tabula rasa the Moderns wished to give the world for a fresh start after the catastrophe of World War I – than the launching ramp for an act of defense against a form of evil. The world of the

fig. 1.4 Aerial photo of the Aula and TU Library Delft
photo: Bedrijfsbureau MMS/TU Delft

Moderns had been transformed from a free, open glassy field of experiment to a world of war. It's hard still to see an optimism in its Brutalism, except in the assumption that the fight is worth fighting. In a world of Mutually Assured Destruction – a serious madness – architecture offered a standing, strong animal form – one of us, sheltering us – ennobled by its obvious determination to resist.

As it aged, the Aula dated, became a dark uncomfortable curiosity, an architecture like so much Brutalism we thought we would never do or need to do again – though we are coming near in animals like the one Jean Nouvel has stabled behind the Rena Sophia in Madrid. But then came the Mecanoo addition, to make a very different sense of it.

The motive of the form of Mecanoo's library addition was an obvious deference, a backing off and staying away, but with a change of spirit that allowed you to enjoy the idea that it was also very intelligently protecting itself from the consequences of being just behind the huge beast. What mattered most was what the addition did with the Modernist ground plane. Mecanoo took the tarmac of the Aula's landing-strip and lifted it up by the edge to find – lo and behold – not the desert of the tabula rasa but space for a cheerful building full of colorful books. Meanwhile the sloping ground plane itself was revealed to be not concrete, but a rich slice of the earth, still to be climbed and walked on, full of possibilities of growth and giving access to new points of view.

The thesis, then, about the public interest in expression – what we learn from old and new architecture – was particularly vivid in the combination. Thus the Aula started off with an argument for the seventies and the Cold War: faced with the horror of existence, we need to hunker down and resist, like Beckett's heroes. In the relative high-seriousness of its times, the bestiality of the Aula is there to animate its resistance and make it heroic. Thirty years later, though, the postmodern mind has the tool of humor to help the Aula get out of bathos and lighten up: now the rocket of resistance is a dunce-cap that shoots out of the ground as if to dramatize what dodos we are if we don't get thinking. And what it shoots through is what we have to get thinking about, the "green" roof of our need to mitigate the effects of building, to manage the damage to the environment done not so much by war as by our self-indulgence.

Hence the lesson of the Aula and its pendant library for an understanding of the public interest in historic preservation. Historic preservation keeps the Aula around to help us remember where we used to be, how we have changed and what we need to do about it. The Aula is real. It's not some spin about the past. It's what quite rightly we used to be afraid of. Now we have new tools, new possibilities and new risks. The lesson of the Aula is not the answers it suggests but the differences it helps us see and the standard it sets for us in addressing what we have to face today. It's the Aula that makes vivid what a wonderful response the Library is for our times.

This was where the work in progress had got as I approached the end of my stay in the reading room. I sped to Delft on my Gazelle on a radiant Sunday morning to get the key illustrative photograph of the Aula and the Library together: no one ever photographs additions from the point of view of what they are added to! Alas, with the help of a still-faster-speeding youth, I wound up without my photograph in the emergency room of the Erasmus Medical Center. Now Agnes Wijers and Joyce Hanssen provided not just friendship, help and excellent company but specific reinforcement for the morale. Aaron and Peter added friendship and Scotch and first-class wine.

The work in progress will ideally hit the shelves in 2007. An early shelf will ideally be at the NAI. In any event, the book will have come into existence – the "opening" that gave rise to its thesis will have occurred – in that short, delicious pause in a long flight of writing in the inspiring light of the NAI.

REFERENCE
– Byard, P.S., The Architecture of Additions: Design and Regulation, New York, W.W. Norton and Company, 1998

central

RALPH KÄMENA

Essay 02

ARCHITECTURE BULLETIN N° 01|2006

The "Central" photographic essay is presented on
pages: 9-10, 19-20, 29-30, 39-42, 51-52, 60-62, 71-72
and on the back flap of this Architecture Bulletin

Ralph Kämena (1968) is an artist who uses photography and photo-animations. The main thread through his work is his perspective on individuals in their relation to their environment. A hallmark of the interiors and urban landscapes he photographs is, as he himself puts it, the physical absence of the person who is nonetheless always present in the traces he or she leaves. The images recall a stage when the actors have just exited.

His photo essay Central deviates in this respect: there are neither interiors nor urban landscapes, and people are anything but absent. Still, he focuses as always on the stage, not on the players. The actors have finished and are about to exit the scene. There is no longer an audience, only the stage itself. Kämena comments on his photo essay as follows: "In Hong Kong, there were such floods of people that I found it necessary to work from an atypical starting point and decided to photograph micro-moments of isolation and absence. I normally frame my subject matter strongly, but this time I refrained from looking through the viewfinder so as to avoid contact. In the flood, you are surrounded by people yet alone."

Martien de Vletter

Tradition and Modernity in the Dutch East Indies

Martien de Vletter (1972) has worked at the Netherlands Architecture Institute since 1997, and has headed the Presentations Department since 2005. She previously did research into architecture and planning in the former Dutch East Indies, with a special focus on the architecture of F.J.L. Ghijsels (1882-1949) and the postwar period in Jakarta. One of her main themes, in this essay as well as in her research, is the quest for identity. In Indonesia this quest is often formulated as seeking a national identity in architecture by endowing the modern Western idiom with characteristically Indonesian features. It is a mistake to dismiss this as exotic romanticism, however. The struggle people have in the Netherlands with non-modernism and traditionalism is the product of similar doubts about identity.

I have taken an intense interest in colonial architecture, and in particular the colonial architecture of Indonesia, since around 1995. The Netherlands Architecture Institute charged me with the task of inventorying the archive of , F.J.L Ghijsels, a Dutch architect who ran one of the most flourishing practices in the former Dutch East Indies, from 1910 to 1929. Inevitably I also became interested in the modern architecture of the 1950s and the decades that followed. All the seminars, symposia, congresses and lectures I have attended since then about contemporary architecture in Indonesia were concerned not only with weighty and profound research topics but also with two more general, and related, questions. What is contemporary Indonesian architecture? And can modern architecture be Indonesian, or is that the sole prerogative of traditional architecture? These questions are with a separate debate on Indonesian identity since independence and on how this identity is linked to the built environment.

To me, these have remained fascinating questions, especially in the context of contemporary architecture. In the Netherlands there is little discussion about whether the work of Mecanoo, MVRDV, Claus & Kaan or Soeters Eldonk Ponec is purely Dutch, neither among modernists nor traditionalists. The importance of the concept, the consultation structure, the design and building process, are important facets of Dutch architecture. But these are not characteristics that only Dutch architects can lay claim to. There is definitely a tradition in Dutch architecture, but I doubt whether any of the firms just mentioned has ever felt inclined or obliged to defend themselves on the issue of whether or not what they do is typically Dutch. The intended location for a project almost always forms a source of inspiration or at least a point of departure for the design, although it is not always obvious in the result. Considering all the international connections and international projects, we may wonder whether there really is such a thing as Dutch architecture.

Today's Indonesian architects continually ask themselves whether what they are doing is truly Indonesian. Building Indonesian architecture is actually considered a criterion of "good" contemporary architecture in Indonesia. This issue overlaps a complicated debate about the terms 'modern' and 'traditional'. It is complicated because not everyone accords the same meanings to these two ostensible opposites. Everyone agrees on the extreme cases of contemporary modern and contemporary traditional construction, but there is a very large gray area between them.

So there is a continual polemic about what "Indonesian" architecture actually means. Among the factors fueling this discussion is the question of what counts as Indonesian architectural heritage. Borobudur is naturally a part of that heritage, as are the remarkable Batak houses of Sumatra (the house has three levels, is supported by piles, and is topped by a soaring roof; livestock is kept under the house, people occupy the middle layer, and ancestor relics hang beneath the eaves). The same is true of the kratons, the Sultans' palaces of Java. But does Indonesia's colonial architecture, whether designed by Dutch or by local architects, also qualify as Indonesian heritage? The nature of Indonesian heritage and Indonesian vernacular traditions, the debates that simmered about them in the 1920s, and their relevance to current discussions form the subject matter of this article.

The dialogue on modern and traditional architecture in Indonesia, on contemporary modernism and traditionalism and how these might play a part in expressing the national identity, is not something new. Dutch and Indonesian architects conducted a lively debate on these issues in the colonial era, in particular between 1910 and 1930. When we reconstruct the discourse of the years between the world wars, it becomes clear that there are many points of similarity with today's discussions.

The core of the 1920s discussion took place between three architects: Thomas Karsten (1884-1945), Henri Maclaine Pont (1884-1971) and Charles Wolff Schoemaker (1882-1949). From the distant platform of the Netherlands, H.P. Berlage also expressed views on the subject although he was not himself active in the East Indies. When the discussion flared up in 1923 it did not come out of the blue, for P.A.J. Moojen and E. Cuypers had already been occupied with these matters some ten years earlier. Indeed, any architect working in the tropics would in fact have asked himself similar questions. The discussion revolved around the question of how "Indonesian" modern architecture could or should be. It arose after the first qualified architects started arriving in the Dutch East Indies around 1900. Their arrival elevated the quality of the architecture and the debate to a higher level. Hitherto it had been mainly civil engineers who had decided how things would be built. The newly arrived young architects, most of them graduates of Delft University of Technology, were searching for a contemporary architectural idiom, much like their colleagues in the Netherlands. The revivalist styles of the nineteenth century no longer satisfied their needs and ideals. The discussion between Karsten, Maclaine Pont and Wolff Schoemaker arose around an abstract question of the nature of Indonesian architecture. To them, the differences in climate and in surroundings presented a challenge. Thomas Karsten was the one who first explicitly raised the issue in an article about an architecture exhibition which was to be held in Semarang in 1920. Although he agreed with Moojen that the arrival of better trained European architects had resulted in improved quality, he believed that the strong link with Europe was not necessarily a guarantee of good architecture:

"The necessary improvement of quality [...] which the more intensive economic life brought with it on a broad front, subsequently had its effect on architecture. Moojen is a name that must be mentioned in this context. At the same time, the first buildings were being completed to designs made in Holland; and the well-known trip to the Indies by the Amsterdam architect Ed. Cuypers, now ten years ago, gives the appearance of having rung in a period of close relations in this area between the Mother Country and the Colony. Surprisingly, however, this is a misapprehension: the Indies has already become too independent for that!"[1]

Karsten observed in the same article that modern architecture in the Indies did not currently present a uniform picture, and he offered an explanation for this:

"On the one hand, a condition for good art and for good architecture is this: inner unity. On the other hand, architecture is bound up with materials, with society, and with temporal and pragmatic possibilities. And in this combination of the desirable and the actual there lies the answer to the question why the Indies is nowadays doomed to confusion in its architecture: the society itself lacks that inner unity. The great rift and the insoluble duality are integral to the essence of the Colony; to the differences of tradition, level of development and intention, between the dominant European elite and the dominated — and now at least struggling to rise up — native society."[2]

The starting points adopted by Karsten, Maclaine Point and Wolff Schoemaker were very different. The importance they attached to the local Javanese building tradition (all three worked mainly on Java) was a significant factor in their differences. Wolff Schoemaker took a functional, formalist approach and hence was least inclined to attach much general importance to traditional Javanese architecture. In his view, it could certainly not provide a basis for a modern architecture. Maclaine Pont had similar doubts but it is clear from the way he posed his questions and from his definition of architecture that he was prepared to ascribe the Javanese architectural tradition a role in the process of achieving a modern architecture.

"Do the Javanese people have an architectural tradition that has emerged from those people themselves and which is a consequence of climactic moments in their history? Do they have an architectural tradition that has moved, and still moves, not only the dominant classes but the entire people, so that the old formal vocabulary can reemerge as a basic element of the newly developing architecture? (...) Do the peoples of Java still have enough of an architecture of their own to enable the new architecture to be connected directly to it? (...) If so, does this architecture satisfy the demands of modern times? And if not, can distinctive changes be introduced within the framework of that architecture, such that it can constitute the best possible architecture for the modern era and a point of departure for the future?"[3]

Maclaine Pont was convinced that there really was such a thing as a Javanese architectural tradition. Archeological studies he had conducted led him to the conclusion that the Hindu-Javanese temples of Central Java could be considered as original Javanese designs in certain respects, since there was an extant Javanese civilization in the era of their building. In a lecture delivered in 1924[4] Maclaine Pont argued that the Sumatrans could not have accomplished the construction of Buddhist shrines (Borobudur, 778-856) in Central Java without the aid of a reasonably civilized Central Javanese population. He found support for this view in that the Javanese drove out the Sumatrans and built a new temple complex themselves only fifty years later (Prambanan, 900-950). An initially unsophisticated population could never have achieved that degree of development in a mere fifty years, Maclain Pont argued.

Wolff Schoemaker held that the origin of the Hindu-Javanese architecture lay in India, and that its execution on Java was a simplified version of the Hindu concept made necessary by the uneducated character of the Javanese labor force. Maclaine Pont countered that this view could not be correct, since a certain system of measurement, the Silpasastra[5], occurred constantly throughout the buildings. Maclaine Pont did not deny the influence of the Indian architecture tradition, but argued that the Javanese applied the originally Indian measurements in such a distinct way that it was reasonable to speak of a truly Javanese development. The continually repeated measurement units of the Silpasastra lent scale to the design and established an aesthetic consonance between different parts of the temple complex. The unit as such did not carry much symbolic or mystical significance, however. Maclaine Pont believed the use of a regular measurement unit on Java was a largely pragmatic choice.

Maclaine Pont's careful research into the reliefs of both Borobudur and Prambanan drew his attention to another important Javanese architectural tradition: the development of the pendopo. A pendopo was originally an open pavilion consisting of characteristic roof supported by columns in a square or rectangular plan. The sloping sides of the pyramid roof have a sharp articulation, with the steeper central part resting on at least four columns. The ceiling of the central section has an ornamentation which depends on the status of the building or its owner. The pendopo forms the public, front part of a traditional Javanese house. Guests are entertained, and feasts and ceremonies take place under the pendopo. Its construction was specific to the Javanese context and differed from that of related structures in other Asian countries. On Java, the wooden roof planes and grilles are an integral part of the construction and afford stability to the central section of the pendopo.

Both Maclaine Pont and Karsten thought the Javanese pendopo could be applied in modern architecture. For Karsten, it was indeed an ideal form:

"In contrast to European buildings, the climax in the spatial effect is achieved in the pendopo entirely by the spatial form itself, independently of any ornamentation, the climax also finding expressing in the exterior though the tall central roof. I consider this an exceptional ex-

fig. 3.1 Savoy Hotel (1939) by
A.F. Albers, Bandung.
photo: Martien de Vletter

fig. 3.2 Pendopo
photo: Harmen van de Wal

fig. 3.3 Villa Isola (1932) by
C.P. de Wolff Schoemaker
photo: Martien de Vletter

ample of a complete unity of form and meaning, of expression and function."[6]

Wolff Schoemaker was also impressed by the tectonic form of the pendopo but disagreed with his colleagues on the structural and technical aspects. Maclaine Pont had conducted much historical and archeological research into the Javanese building forms and had looked carefully into how the roof was built. The structure obtains its rigidity from the way the horizontal rafters were joined. The roof framework is strong and can support considerable weight, which Maclain Pont saw as its advantage. He demonstrated that this technique minimized the amount of material needed and thus economized on wood. To Wolff Schoemaker the latter seemed illogical, for the whole island was forested so there was no reason at all for the Javanese to be thrifty with wood.

Another point Maclaine Pont stressed on several occasions, was his concern about the rapidity with which the traditional knowledge of Javanese architecture was being lost, because buildings were increasingly designed by a central agency in Batavia. Wolff Schoemaker agreed to some extent with this concern and thought that the best traditions were certainly worthy of being preserved. However, he wished to protect the Javanese architecture from obsolete practices and to modernize the indigenous vernacular by the applying the knowledge of European architecture. This was perhaps where the widest gulf lay between Wolff Schoemaker and the others. Maclaine Pont and Karsten thought Javanese architecture was an extremely good starting point for the development of a modern architecture, whereas Wolff Schoemaker hoped to create an improved, modern tropical architecture style using Western architectural principles:

"A question in which the architects in Indonesia still show too little interest is the possibility of developing a European style in architecture, a style in which the tropical character is more fully expressed. While the architectural products of cultured Northern countries are already showing more and more common and related traits, characteristically for a consolidating style, a strong subjectivism and formal eclecticism still predominates in Indonesia."[7]

This statement nonetheless indicates that the architects had something in common. They all appeared to agree that the historicizing styles of the nineteenth century were no longer satisfactory, and that research was necessary. That Wolff Schoemaker was equally convinced of this is clear from another passage in the same article:

"The Indo-European architect must study the Indonesian works, to immerse himself in them in the same way as our first rationalists studied medieval architecture, if he is to comprehend the essence of this art and find new impetus in it."[8]

Although the architects concurred that research was needed into the historic buildings, their opinions remained divided over the usability of that knowledge. Maclaine Pont sought to penetrate the essence of Javanese architecture, which he thought a highly usable design basis for modern buildings, as he demonstrated in his design for the Polytechnic in Bandung. Karsten drew primarily on the pendopo form in his designs. How Wolff Schoemaker put his knowledge of historical architecture research to use is unclear, however. It would seem that he was unable to apply his knowledge in formal design, as though he did not trust it; for Wolff Schoemaker had warned several times that the architect must be on his guard against "sticking" Indonesian style elements onto primarily Western architecture. *"It is wrong to think that the use of ornaments of pseudo-Indonesian character and the use of shapes based on Asian examples will lead to a solution for a building in tropical style. It is especially wrong to pursue that solution by deriving forms not from the products of a unified stylistic culture, but from products found in illustrations from diverse Oriental countries and from differing periods — forms whose significance is not understood, forms which unless interpreted in a consistent fashion will distract from one another and produce disunited accents in the building. Only a true understanding of foreign forms will put one in a position to transform their essential traits, without danger, into new motifs and to dispose them tactfully in a harmonious connection."* [9]

Maclaine Pont and Karsten must have concurred with this standpoint. They too thought that the inappropriate use of ornaments and structural solutions would result in a poor kind of tropical architecture. Yet Maclaine Pont was accused of doing just that by Wolff Schoemaker when the latter expressed his opinion about the design for the Bandung Polytechnic. In his view, the Polytechnic Buildings, where he himself worked, were inconsistent with the surrounding landscape, for the design was in the Minangkabau style (from Sumatra) and thus misplaced on Java. The architect's determination to adapt the building to its environment, he maintained, was greater than his knowledge of how to do so.

The discussion between the three Dutch architects in the East Indies was thus primarily about the question of how native motifs and circumstances could play a part in modern architecture. There was also the question of whether it was right to apply the different architectural traditions of the islands of the ar-chipelago indiscriminately; the very origins of these "typically Indonesian building traditions" were regarded rather skeptically.

The result for Indonesian architecture was that prestigious buildings such as office blocks, ministries and banks were largely built in an "official" modern architecture. The style was modern, but the structural methods used made allowance for the climate, while local ornamental motifs, in the form of wood carving or other detailed work, appeared only sporadically. For housing, the same architects also built in a modern idiom but incorporated many more local features into the structure, the detailing and the floor plans. They took this tendency even farther in the case of schools and hospitals. Local materials, motifs, structural options and plans all appeared more frequently than they did in other types of building. The less formal the function, the more "Indonesian" the architecture became. As we shall soon see, this classification is still relevant today.

The first ruler of the Republic of Indonesia, President Sukarno (1901-1970) was himself an architect. He wished to avoid any references to history, either oriental or occidental. His ideology and his style of leadership of the newborn nation implied adopting the same architectural idiom as was prevalent among many of his Western colleagues: the International Style. Brasilia, designed by Oscar Niemeyer, was his shining example. The buildings in International Style that rose up in all the cities of Indonesia in the nineteen fifties were meant to proclaim the new identity. In effect they were a statement that the new nation could hold its head high in international circles, as demonstrated by their modern architecture which was as fresh and contemporary as the nation itself. One of the most attractive designs from that period is an office block by the American architect Paul Rudolph. His building was designed to stay cool without the benefit of air conditioning. Using traditional means, such as wide eaves and natural ventilation, he succeeded in making a modern building.

President Suharto, who succeeded Sukarno in 1966, broke away from the latter's International Style preferences. This development again paralleled trends in other areas of the world. By the late sixties and early seventies, people were beginning to feel dissatisfied with the International Style, and functionalist urban design was falling out of favor. A postmodern architecture emerged in many countries. The mainstream of this movement was thinly represented in the Netherlands, although a revived interest and respect for history resulted a more moderate but widespread variant. The same was true in Indonesia. Postmodernism did not make much of a physical impact until much later there, at the time of the Pacific Rim boom of the mid nineties. Suharto took a considerable interest in Indonesian history, and a significant concern of his was to cultivate an inclusive Indonesian identity, in which both history and architecture would play an important part. One of the most notable achievements in this area has been Jakarta's open air museum of architecture, Taman Mini. With its replicas of vernacular styles from all over the archipelago, it has become a popular tourist attraction. However, promoting local architectural tradition does not necessarily imply building straightforward imitations of traditional examples. It means respecting aspects of traditional form that are still vital and perhaps incorporating them as quotations in modern buildings.

A complication of the contemporary discourse on tradition and modernity in Indonesia is that a non-indigenous layer was already superimposed on local traditional styles during the colonial period. This situation is not of course unique. The Netherlands too has "borrowed" traditions from other cultures in the past. In Indonesia, however, the mixture of disparate elements continues to add friction to the debate on contemporary, 21st century architecture. In particular there is continuing disagreement about whether colonial architecture really can be counted as part of the Indonesian cultural heritage and hence as part of the Indonesian identity and tradition. My view is that while this architecture is not "typically" Indonesian (after all, is Borobudur typically Indonesian?) it does form part of Indonesia's cultural heritage (rather like Richard Meier's city hall in The Hague which over a period of fifty years has gained a status as Dutch heritage even though designed by an American).

Indonesia's ongoing discussion on the use of traditional architecture is not unique. As in the Netherlands and countless other countries, most people (the bourgeois majority) are fond

fig. 3.4 International Style
photo: Martien de Vletter

fig. 3.5 Hospital in Bandung,
AIA Bureau
photo: Martien de Vletter

fig. 3.6 Kebayoran (1955)
photo: Martien de Vletter

of traditional architecture. In Holland it is a house in 1930s style. The Indonesians also like the thirties look but ancient Greek and Roman models are just as popular; indeed it is sometimes quite unclear whicht tradition the designs actually refer to. As in 1925, too, formal buildings are principally built in a contemporary international style, and the less formal the project the more traditional ingredients may be included in the design.

Is that so bad? I don't think so, although I would find it interesting if a greater weight were given to local context in the design. I mean not so much historicist quotations of tradition, but a response to the locus, warts and all; perhaps in the same way as the ING Building by Meijer & Van Schooten stands on legs just tall enough to peek over the Amsterdam circular; or in the way MVRDV turns a problem into an advantage in their wozoco apartments, or abstracts traditional features and takes them to extremes in their houses on Hageneiland.

FOOTNOTES

1 Karsten, Th., "Bij de ie Indiese Architektuurtentoonstelling", in De Taak, March 13 1920, p. 303.

2 Karsten, Th., De Taak, March 13 1920, p. 302.

3 Maclaine Pont, H., Djawa, 1923, p. 117.

4 This lecture was published in Maclaine Pont, H., "De betekenis der Middeleeuwsche monumenten op Java" in Djawa 1924, p. 199-238.

5 A Silpasastra is a system of rules with religious connotations, from Southern India. The tala was a unit of length equivalent to 12 angulas. An angula was one quarter of a musti, which was the size of a hand's breadth, about 240 mm. This corresponded to the distance between the extremities of the thumb and middle finger of the stretched hand.

6 Karsten, Th., "De waarde van de latere Javaansche bouwkunst", in Djawa, 1925, p. 208.

7 Wolff Schoemaker, C.P., "Indische bouwkunst en de ontwikkeling smogelijkheid van een Indo-Europeeschen architectuurstijl", in Indisch Bouwkundig Tijdschrift, 31 May 1923, p. 188.

8 Wolff Schoemaker, C.P., 31 May 1923, p. 191.

9 Wolff Schoemaker, C.P., 31 May 1923, p. 190.

A Forgotten Architectural Theory

Nineteenth-century Eclecticism and the (Post)Modern

GEERT PALMAERTS

Essay 04

ARCHITECTURE BULLETIN N° 01|2006

"Dans les cours des transitions sociales, l'histoire entière le démontre, l'architecture fait de l'éclectisme."

"In times of social transition, as all history demonstrates, architecture turns to eclecticism."

César Daly, "Ingénieurs et Architectes", *Revue Générale de l'Architecture*, 1877.

Prologue

Architectural theory only ever covers a fraction of public space. Nevertheless, in the fifth edition of *The Language of Post-Modern Architecture*, Charles Jencks defines the postmodern movement in contemporary architecture as "an eclectic mix of traditional or local codes with Modern ones." [1] This description and Jencks's argument in favor of eclecticism represents a striking position in twentieth-century architectural theory. Jencks, like the protagonists of New Urbanism, openly dares to propagate eclecticism following decades in which architects and architectural historians have utterly condemned it. To support his case he refers to one of his own designs in which extant, native motifs are combined with prefab elements and traditional roofing. This mixture of the old, the new and the regional has come to be known as "Radical Eclecticism."

Geert Palmaerts (1972) studied philosophy and art history at Katholieke Universiteit Leuven. He took a doctorate at Vrije Universiteit Amsterdam in 2005 with a thesis on nineteenth-century eclecticism. Geert Palmaerts is currently engaged in postdoctoral work at the University of Groningen, where he is researching the aspect of Bildung in the architecture theory of the first half of the twentieth century. Now that the postmodern vogue has subsided in the Netherlands as elsewhere, and the word eclecticism is heard more and more often, it seems that the word is not always used precisely. What is eclecticism really about, and what does it mean to us today?

But what is eclecticism? The notion stems from the Greek terms *ek legein* and *eklegasthai*, which refer to choosing, selecting, picking out. According to the *New Oxford Dictionary of English*, eclectic means "deriving ideas, style or taste from a broad and diverse range of sources". Eclecticism was especially widespread in the nineteenth century when many architects used a range of different motifs in their designs. These were often historical, although exotic motifs, taken from Moorish or Chinese cultures for example, were also used. It is therefore quite logical that contemporary postmodernism should show an interest in nineteenth-century architecture. New Urbanism is inspired by urban planning ideas that preceded

Le Corbusier's *Urbanisme* of 1925. An interest in Ildefons Cerdà, designer of the nineteenth-century expansion of Barcelona, and in his treatise *Teoría General de la Urbanización* (1867), also fits these tendencies.[3]

It is striking that, amid this reorientation, the theoretical background of nineteenth-century eclecticism is only superficially understood. Jencks, for example, makes use of a questionable interpretation of the "weak eclecticism of the past", which barely differs from that of the modern predecessors he criticizes. The "Radical Eclecticism" that is subsequently presented as new is – apparently without Jencks being aware of it – almost a replica of the nineteenth-century version.[4] Those who wish to champion a contemporary eclecticism – and those who adamantly oppose it – could do worse than to refer back to their nineteenth-century colleagues. Not only did they have similar debates, but the themes that nineteenth-century eclectics addressed in their heatedly contested architectural theories are still relevant today.

In this essay I would like to dust off two such themes: the notion of liberty which runs through eclecticism, and the related understanding of beauty. It is not my intention to correct the postmodernists or the New Urbanists on their architectural history, but I do believe that the controversy surrounding modern, postmodern and historicizing architecture might benefit from a more accurate historical perspective. It might be helpful to look back to the period in which the debate about modern architecture began, going even further back than the origin of twentieth-century Modernism. Beneath the layer of dusty styles – an image held up to us by many an historiographer of eclecticism – lies a carefully constructed theory of architecture. This theory has largely been forgotten, but the points of departure and "modern" reactions to nineteenth-century eclecticism have molded our thinking on architecture right up to the present day.

De la Liberté dans l'Art:
The Notion of Liberty in Eclecticism

Today's ignorance of eclecticism is largely due to a modernist writing of history. Sigfried Giedion, Nikolaus Pevsner and Henry-Russell Hitchcock wrote the history of architecture from the viewpoint of the victors, as Arthur Drexler aptly put it in his book *The Architecture of the École des Beaux-Arts*.[5] Giedion and his followers sympathized with and were a part of the Modern Movement, from which their negative attitude towards eclecticism stemmed. They emphasized only the decadence and impotence which, they believed, marked nineteenth-century architecture. In the first edition of *Space, Time and Architecture* published in 1941, Giedion stated that "eclecticism smothered all creative energy" – an image which has since proved almost indelible.[6] The difference was defined as one between modern and traditional: new twentieth-century architecture versus old-fashioned, nineteenth-century architecture, with eclecticism placed almost entirely in the latter category. A large section of architectural history adopted this antithesis and as a consequence almost no independent research into eclecticism has been carried out. Eclecticism was simply that which modern architecture had pushed aside. But what lies concealed beneath the term "modern architecture" and, more importantly, is this antithesis as self-evident as it seems?

From the 1890s onward, modern architecture primarily meant emphasizing the rational principle of architecture. It was then that it became modern for architecture to respond to the demands of construction and visible structure. This movement drew its design and aesthetics from a renewed interest in rationalism. However, the eclectics held a different view: they used historical motifs as additions to their designs and believed architecture was losing its power of expression due to a one-sided focus on rationalism. In the words of the founder of the Deutsch Werkbund, Hermann Muthesius, himself indebted to the eclecticism of his day: "we use styles like a language, as it were, a language in which we express architectural concepts that are specific to us and to the present".[7] That this view is resurfacing in postmodern architecture is borne out by Jencks's observations on language and semantics, which he ascribes to contemporary eclecticism.[8] Postmodernism criticizes Modernism's inability to communicate and no longer attaches importance to the dichotomy between modern and traditional. Contemporary intellectuals like Jencks and the New Urbanists turn away from a uniform design practice which they find restrictive.

The nineteenth-century eclectics felt very strongly about the notion of liberty. César Daly, the French architecture theorist and editor-in-chief of *Revue Générale de l'Architecture* (1840 – 1890), steadily worked out the theme of eclectic design freedom.

Influenced by his contemporary, the philosopher Victor Cousin, he explicitly defined eclecticism as being both an architectural theory *and* a contemporary cultural phenomenon. The ignorance of Daly's work that prevails today is somewhat undeserved: he was as famous in his day as Viollet-le-Duc and we cannot afford to ignore him if we are to achieve a better understanding of nineteenth-century eclecticism.[9]

The first important period in the formation of eclecticism was 1840 to 1860. This was when Daly contrasted eclecticism to the design practice of the École des Beaux-Arts and the Neo-Gothic. Although eclectics had often been educated in the department of architecture at the École des Beaux-Arts, they opposed its predilection for Greek or Roman examples, which they considered too limiting. In the newly emerging search for a nineteenth-century means of expression, classicism was accused of generating a message that was too restrictive and based on an antiquated model of knowledge and design. It was no longer considered opportune for architects to be educated in a theory of architecture and design that denied the demands of a new modernity. The emergence of new typologies such as railway stations, the rediscovery of the national past, and the socio-political changes that were taking place, complicated thinking on architecture in the first few decades of the nineteenth century and precluded a uniform approach. Eclecticism fitted this context perfectly. It was, in the words of César Daly, a "new school which does not limit the power of its imagination to reproducing sacred monuments from whichever historical era they may come from (...) this new school studies the unknown powers of the masterpieces of all eras, but, above all, it wants to be the expression of its own time."[10]

In France in particular, eclectic architects consequently engaged themselves with liberal and socially utopian groups. In the first half of the nineteenth century, eclecticism was a social movement allied to political forces that sought a new state order in post-revolutionary France. The philosopher and politician, Victor Cousin, who presented himself as an eclectic, was often the spider in the web. His liberal eclecticism was actively acknowledged in politics and (state) education as well as in art circles, where avant-garde journals such as *Le Globe* disseminated *éclectisme moderne*. The eclecticism of the first half of the nineteenth century was unmistakably a progressive movement.

In terms of architectural theory, this progressive attitude was summarized and consolidated in César Daly's manifesto "De la Liberté dans l'Art" (1847-1949). This little known text represents an initial phase in a polemic on style that lasted many decades. The demand that arose for new thinking on architecture led to the question of how buildings should be built and in which style. As stated, the eclectics considered the classicism of the École des Beaux-Arts to be wholly inappropriate, because to them it was a form of expression of a specific historical context. The same applied to Neo-Gothic: the eclectics, like today's postmodernists, stressed the contextual nature of all forms of design and consequently argued for all motifs to be used freely.

This matter was expressed succinctly in 1845, when the architect Franz-Christian Gau presented a Neo-Gothic design for a church in Paris based on Cologne's Gothic cathedral. The board of the École des Beaux-Arts published a diatribe against the design, entitled *Considérations sur la question de savoir s'il est convenable au XIXe siècle de bâtir des églises en style gothique* (1845). The board rejected the Gothic style as being inappropriate for the nineteenth-century, which in turn led to reactions in *Annales archéologiques*, the journal of the Neo-Gothic school. A number of architects, including August Maine with his "Essai sur l'Architecture Religieuse au XIXe Siècle" (1849), then proposed an eclectic design solution in the *Revue Générale*, including. It was against this background that Daly decided to champion the freedom of eclecticism in "De la Liberté dans l'Art". As well as three articles, a provocative illustration, "L'Architecture Contemporaine", was also published in 1849. This drawing by the architect Victor Ruprich-Robert visualized eclecticism's belief in progress. The figure of Architectura was presented as "art nouveau" enthroned upon a locomotive, the symbol of the most progressive technology. The locomotive moves forward across an even ground bearing references to all kinds of styles, from Gothic to Byzantine and Persian. This eclectic notion of progress is contrasted with a satirical representation of the adherents of Classicism and the Neo-Gothic who are stuck in polemics and the reproduction of monuments such as the Theater of Marcellus and Chartres cathedral. On the edge of the illustration and in the articles, Daly quoted contemporary artists, intellectuals and politicians who, in his view, propagated the new, nineteenth-century notion of liberty, including Victor Hugo and the liberal politician Ludovic Vitet. The quote from Abel Villeman, lecturer in literature at the Sorbonne and friend of Victor Cousin, is particularly telling: "We are eclectic in the sense that we love all that is beautiful, ingenious and new, regardless of which school it belongs to."[11] What Daly wanted to demonstrate with these quotes was that, to him, eclecticism was an unavoidable consequence of a more complex social order. This was the expression of his belief in the link between society and architectural progress: the new complexity of nineteenth-century society meant it should utilize different forms of knowledge and, consequently, along with nineteenth-century architecture, was unavoidably eclectic.

Truth, Beauty and Function: Nineteenth-century Nonsense?

Eclecticism was, therefore, more than impotent historicism. Like postmodernism, it resisted an all too-uniform-design code. It also contained a specific notion of beauty. The eclectics believed that any effect could be achieved through individualistic freedom in design, and that stylistic expression could be adapted to specific contexts and tasks. This by no means only occurred in terms of historicism; polychromy and decoration were also additions to an otherwise often plain architecture. The triumvirate of "beauty", "truth" and "function" – the wheels of progress – were complementary. Starting from the aesthetics of the day, such as those of Victor Cousin, the eclectics employed their own interpretation of the Vitruvian schema *venustas*, *firmitas* and *utilitas*. Truth, beauty and function each represented a part of ar-

chitecture, not because these qualities are inherent in architecture, but because the eclectics saw architecture as an expression of human possibility: it is people who build and they build according to their capabilities. Humans are rational, but they are also emotional and need comfort. A truly complete architecture should represent all these values and cannot be built solely according to rational terms. Architecture, therefore, has an instinctive quality, just like people. Historical motifs served this position, but it also explains the floral motifs on the cast-iron pillars, polychromy, and ultimately the evocative whiplash style of Art Nouveau. However ridiculous all this might seem, it was an essential part of nineteenth-century architectural aesthetics and fundamentally different from the rationalism that was emerging.

The rationalism that became popular among a minority of architects from the 1860s onward, was critical of this notion of beauty. Eclectic architecture was dishonest and an architecture of façade, because it looked for extra design beyond the construction itself. These architects assigned greater importance to the notion of truth: true architecture was sober and displayed the construction in all its honesty. Architectural truth became a moral category and decoration, in Adolf Loos's vision for example, became a crime. This outlook formed an important starting point for thinking on architecture in the twentieth century. It is still seen as the route to modernism and has shaped a historical account in terms of an evolution of quality.[12] Yet this history is incomplete. It is based on criticisms voiced by a distinct group of architects and fails to acknowledge that the eclectics had a different approach to architecture. Eclecticism was far more than building in styles, and eclectics too were rationalists. *Le Vrai*, Truth, was one of the wheels on Architectura's locomotive, alongside Beauty and Function (*Le Beau* and *L'Utile*). The supporting elements of eclectically designed buildings were rarely concealed and the use of modern innovations such as glass or cast iron was very frequent. Despite the pressure of standardization and industrialization, the eclectics refused to accept that rationalism alone could generate a fully-fledged architecture.

Is the eclectic standpoint of the nineteenth century now largely obsolete? Of course, especially when twentieth-century architecture at times has shown itself to be not purely rational. Emotion in architecture, or the lack of it in certain modernist architecture, is still a topic of discussion and it returns in postmodernism and particularly New Urbanism. It also perhaps explains the success of historicizing architecture among a large section of the public. Modernism was always quick to denounce members of a disobliging public as laymen, but to analyze this from an eclectic, rather than a rationalist standpoint, we have to ask whether our architecture is complete and flexible enough? Do we review architecture often enough from an anthropological perspective? What does architecture in which people feel at home look like? This represents a vacuum in contemporary architectural theory which is rapidly being filled by New Urbanism and developers with a nose for the style of the 1930s.

To my mind, this vacuum is caused by a one-sided appeal to a modernity that no longer exists, to a "modern" architecture that is perhaps primarily an ideological construct. A reconsideration of what preceded it might

fig. 4   "L'Architecture Contemporaine" (1849, drawing by Victor Ruprich-Robert), Revue Générale de L'Architecture et des Travaux Publics, [8] (1849–50), fig. 18.

be worthwhile: what have we given up and what could be added? The forgotten debate between eclectics and rationalists in the last decades of the nineteenth century might well turn out to be extraordinarily relevant today.

FOOTNOTES

1 Charles Jencks, The Language of Post-Modern Architecture, London, 1987, p. 133: "Post-Modern architecture, in an attempt to communicate, is double-coded, an eclectic mix of traditional or local codes with Modern ones."

2 Charles Jencks, The Language of Post-Modern Architecture, London, 1987, p. 128.

3 Michael Hebbert, "New Urbanism – the Movement in Context", Built Environment, (29) 3, 2003, 193 – 209.

4 Charles Jencks, The Language of Post-Modern Architecture, London, 1987, p. 129.

5 Arthur Drexler, "Preface and Acknowledgements", in Arthur Drexler (ed.), The Architecture of the École des Beaux-Arts, London, 1977, p. 6: "We think we know what modern architecture is (...) and how it differs from what preceded it; but we are no longer so certain as to what it should become and how it should be taught. And since history is written by the victors, the literature of the modern movement has helped to perpetuate confusion as to what was lost."

6 Sigfried Giedion, Space, Time and Architecture, London, 1961 (1941), p. 292: "Eclecticism smothered all creative energy. Here and there – especially as the century wore on – voices were raised in protest, but they could do nothing to alter conditions (a) not a single one managed to escape from the atmosphere of eclecticism."

7 Hermann Muthesius, Kultur und Kunst, Jena, 1909, 2. ed., p. 135: "Wir brauchen die Stile sozusagen als Sprache, mit der wir unsere eignen, der Gegenwart angemessenen architektonischen Gedanken aussprechen."

8 Charles Jencks, The Language of Post-Modern Architecture, London, 1987, p. 129: "Unlike Modernism, it makes use of the full spectrum of communicational means – metaphorical and symbolic as well as spatial and formal. Like traditional eclecticism it selects the right style, or subsystem, where it is appropriate."

9 Richard Becherer, Science plus Sentiment. César Daly's Formula for Modern Architecture, Ann Arbor, Michigan, 1984; Geert Palmaerts, Eclecticisme. Over moderne architectuur in de negentiende eeuw, Rotterdam, 2005; Marc Saboya, Presse et architecture au XIXe siècle. César Daly et la Revue Générale de l'Architecture et des Travaux Publics, Paris, 1991.

10 César Daly, "Monument de Juillet élevé sur la place de la Bastille", Revue Générale de l'Architecture et des Travaux Publics I (1840), 758: "Ce monument doit attirer l'attention des artistes pour plus d'une raison. Sa composition est conforme aux principes de cette nouvelle école qui n'étend pas limiter son imagination à la reproduction de monuments consacrés de quelque époque qu'ils soient du passé (a) cette nouvelle école étudie les secrets ressorts des chefs-d'oeuvre de tous les siècles, mais, avant tout, elle veut être l'expression du sien."

11 César Daly, "De la Liberté dans L'Art. À Monsieur Ludovic Vitet", RGA 7 (1847/48), 400: "Villemain – (a) Nous sommes éclectiques en ce sens que nous aimons tout ce qui est beau, ingénieux, nouveau, n'importe quelle soit l'école."

12 A recent example: Werner Oechslin, Otto Wagner, Adolf Loos and the Road to Modern Architecture, Cambridge, 2002.

The Sentiments of Architecture

JAN HOOGSTAD

Essay 05

ARCHITECTURE BULLETIN N° OI | 2006

The nice thing about looking back is that you can see the road you've taken. This standpoint gives you an opportunity to develop a set of ideas about what was and what ought to be. In other words, retrospection enables you to form a clear idea about the future. That's what I have tried to do here.

In the half century I've been working as an architect, I have increasingly come to realize that rationalism has become the norm in architecture, and hence one of its most dangerous enemies. This is a far-reaching thesis and it needs substantiating. Nonetheless it doesn't come out of nowhere, but issues from a deeply felt awareness of the essence of architecture. For me this essence consists of the following elements:

– The great themes of architecture – spatial impact and appearance – make an appeal to our emotions.
– The most important emotions for architecture are: the sense of seclusion, joy and security. These are in turn linked with identity and recognition.
– Experiencing, and enjoying, architecture is a matter of feelings.

In my view, the emotional experience of architecture is an essential and indispensable element in and for our profession. And I think that involving the atmospheric and the emotional in the design

Jan Hoogstad (1930) has been working in his own firms and partnerships since 1957. He established Hoogstad Architecten in 1991, changing the name to Ector Hoogstad Architecten in January 2006. His best known building is the Ministry of VROM (Housing, Spatial Planning and the Environment) in The Hague, built in 1992. As a visiting lecturer, his courses and presentations often deal with the relation between the experiencing of space and time, and with the principle that architecture shapes not only space but society. An example was his animated talk on "The Sentiments of Architecture", a lecture delivered on January 12, 2006 as part of the ARCHITECT@NAI series. Last year, Hoogstad broke a lance for his concept of "atmospheric" architecture, in a lecture in Nagoya, Japan. He has merged the content of these two lectures specially for this first issue of Architecture Bulletin.

process leads to buildings in which human beings come into their own. Architecture is of great value as a means of experiencing our existence. Before anything else, an architect is a creator of atmospheres. But one wonders whether architects realize this. And whether they are capable any longer of fulfilling their prime role of creators of atmospheres.

Perfect process, perfect building?

Looking at present-day architecture, I'm inclined to think that they aren't. What's going wrong then? And where? In my opinion, the reason they've lost their way has to do with what I call the "legacy of rationalism".

Design briefs are approached in a way that is extremely objective and logical. The emphasis is on function. And on cost management. There is no room for considerations of feelings, atmospheres and emotions. I can best clarify this with a diagram.

Schedules like these have been employed ever since "professional" management swooped down on planning processes – roughly, that is, since the new city hall building in Amsterdam, the Stopera, notoriously exceeded its budgets. Time is laid out horizontally and the types of work to be carried out are ordered vertically. It is an analytical process that begins with the work of dissecting the brief. After that, one proceeds to surface analyses and relational sche-

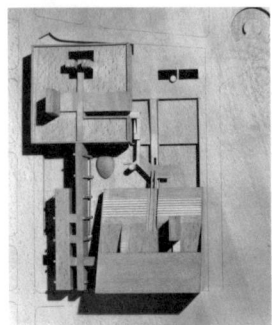

fig. 5.1   Centre Pompidou

mas; budgets are then drawn up and structural designs are produced. All of these are laid out linearly on a time scale and end when the building is delivered.

If this process is implemented flawlessly – with every stage of the planning and construction process getting the required attention – the result is a perfect building. But the process does not guarantee that this building will be architecturally interesting, or even a good building – one with a 'happy atmosphere' for instance. Any aspirations in this direction usually disappear under a welter of prevailing economic interests. Users often call buildings that have come about in this supposedly perfect fashion "frigid" and "distant". Recently I even came across the term "autistic architecture".

Poetic Thinking

I don't want to detract at all from the planning schedule. It's a useful aid and it ensures that you don't overlook anything. But I think that prior to the rational process you need to think about the question of what sort of building you want to make, of the atmosphere that should permeate it. I've gradually come to the conclusion that thinking about atmospheres, let alone giving any account of them, is still in its stone age period. Compared with hard, measurable factors such as time and money, the issue of atmosphere is soft and vulnerable. It is fragile and easily comes off worst in any rationally organized planning process. The problem is that speeches about atmosphere are liable to be interpreted as 'merely' poetic and are easy to dismiss as 'woolly-minded'. In the management camp the rational side of the planning process automatically gets a hearing, so that rationalism pretty much always gets the upper hand.

fig. 5.2   Jungerhans Tower

Of course what is involved is an entirely different modes of thought. Rational thought is linear (consistent), causal (cause and consequence) and concrete. It requires expertise. It is the mode of thought we employ to manufacture buildings and automobiles. Poetic thinking by contrast is more a way of thinking in fields of ideas or three-dimensional images. It also means thinking about our image of architecture. And hence about the question of what atmosphere can best serve both the building and its users. Is it – to mention just one pair of polar opposites – to be an "exuberant-extravert" structure or a "restrained and introvert" one?

At the level of the individual too there is a distinction between rational and poetic thought. The two thought processes take place in different areas of our brains. Rational thought occurs in the neo-cortex, the domain of control, while the seat of atmospheric thought is the limbic system, the realm of emotions and feelings. The former thinks in terms of connections, the latter, the mode of atmosphere and poetry, in proportions. The former is linear, the latter associative.

fig. 5.3   Poemé Music Theatre
Enschede

Architecture is the Loser

My own objection to rationalism as it has evolved in architecture is that architectural rationalism ignores the importance of poetry. I think that poetry has only itself to blame for this. It has never really claimed its place and thus it has not been allocated any recognized spot in the building process. And this is a huge omission and loss. Rationalism has become an end in itself. In the best case scenario, atmospheric/poetic thought hitches a ride like a sort of stowaway. And somewhere its presence is genuinely missed. People today often try to stick the element of feeling on retrospectively, as a sort of gimmick. It is both surrogate and an afterthought. The result is an architecture of the spectacle that makes it abundantly clear that by then it is too late to do any good. In the end we have lost the essence of architecture.

Human beings exist in space. And three-dimensional space can only be captured in atmospheric images. I am convinced that knowing *where* you are expands one's sense of existence. It is a quality of architecture that, as a spatial system, it can offer us that sense of security and identification. It can give us the feeling of having a place we can call our own. And hence also our sense of the difference between large and small. The need to delimit space in order to experience it is present at the birth of architecture. But this awareness is no longer our point of departure.

As a result the answer to the question, "where am I?" ceases to be the province of architecture. I think that the answer to this question is at least as important as that to the question of "what am I?". In conjunction these questions and answers lead us to the ultimate question, namely, "who am I?". Not only does architectural space make us aware of where we are; it also expands our thinking. Architectural space forms the context for what happens in it. The context sets the tone for what happens in the space.

Human Beings as Creators of Spheres

In his book "Spheres"(2003), the German philosopher Peter Sloterdijk states that human beings are, above all, creators of spheres. Human beings must give form to the immensity of the world. Thus we surround ourselves with what Sloterdijk calls "spheres". The German word *sphäre* can either mean "sphere" or "atmosphere", and Sloterdijk uses it in both senses. These may consist of a house, a plot of land, a park, a nationality or nation. We do this to protect ourselves against the others and against the world – against its immensity. But we also do it to create a small-scale imitation of the immeasurable world.

According to Sloterdijk, the question of our "where" is more meaningful than ever before. Maybe even more meaningful than that of our "what". We have to focus on the spot that people create in order to be what and who they are. This place is what Sloterdijk means by a "sphere". A sphere is the intimate, enclosed, shared "circle" that humans dwell in, in as much as they succeed in being human. Because right from the start, the creation of spheres – both small and large –

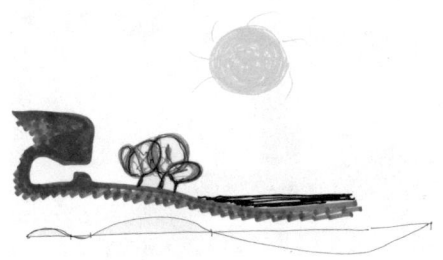

fig. 5.4 Cross section of house

means that humans are creatures that create worlds around them. And who look towards horizons. Living in spheres, Sloterdijk says, means producing a dimension one can comprehend. Spheres are spatial creations that function as immune systems for ecstatic creatures who feel "the outside" act upon themselves. Space – the bounded space in an architectural sense – can give us the idea that we dispose of a very small plot that seemingly, exists separately from the immensity of infinity.

Sloterdijk's philosophy impacts on my ideas about the meaning of space. I am referring to the space that offers seclusion or security, but also to the space that offers openness and freedom. And also to that which conjures up one's ties to materials, the space that links one with light, that challenges one to interaction or chance encounters. But I always see space as the unifying context for the events that occur in it.

The New Functionalism

The question of what architecture is really about has always preoccupied me – perhaps unconsciously and certainly against my best interests. Because I also learned very early on that architecture needed to be "useful" or "functional".

At the time when I was being educated there was no room for atmospheres or questions such as "who am I?" and "where am I?" It was just after the Second World War – the age when rationalism and functionalism reigned supreme. My teachers were architects such as Rietveld, Vordemberge-Gildewart, Van den Broek and Maaskant. Men who in their turn were strongly influenced by Martin Gropius, Marcel Breuer and Mies van der Rohe.

I recall that I organized a series of extra-curricular lectures in my student years (1952-1958) as the chairperson of the "X-function" student society. We were acutely aware of the social significance of architecture. We felt that it deserved all the support it could get in the revival of functionalism that was stimulated by the post-war reconstruction period.

It was in the period that Van Tijen and Maaskant designed the Groothandelsgebouw, Van de Broek and Bakema the Lijnbaan shopping street and Marcel Breuer the Bijenkorf department store – all projects in Rotterdam. Their lectures and classes had a huge impact on our development. We seized the opportunity to invite Marcel Breuer to give a lecture. Initially he agreed, but when he asked us to propose a subject for the lecture and we came up with "The New Functionalism Today, its Future Development and its Shortcomings" – and that was the last we heard of him.

The Taste of Herring

Much later, in 1974, I met Breuer again. I was the building standards member of the Rotterdam Council inner city committee. Breuer defended his plan for a car park as an extension to the Bijenkorf. The plan got a lot of flak from the committee that consisted of Bodon, Jo van de Broek, J.P. Kloos and Maaskant, with Salomonson

fig. 5.5 House on the Westerkade, Rotterdam

idem fig. 5.6

and Apon and myself as rising stars. The criticism amounted to little more than whether you should build a car park with sloping floors in a context where all the building floors were horizontal. The argument went that in a city with horizontal floors, a multistory car park with floors like a ramp simply didn't fit. The fear was that it would result in a form of *trompe l'oeil* with existing floors in the neighborhood looking as though they were sloping or had subsided while those of the car park were horizontal.

The plan risked being rejected by a majority. Maaskant was for it and, like a coward, I had abstained. When Van de Broek asked Maaskant what he thought was so beautiful about this plan, Maaskant said: "Jo, I can't explain to you what a herring tastes like." In other words, beauty is not something you can explain in words.

Breuer, who had been invited to explain his plan, exploded with rage about such nonsense. He rose and, propping his considerable weight with both hands on the table, bellowed in a stentorian voice, "I am a lifetime of architecture!" With that he let us know that he wasn't just "something", but also "someone". That put a stop to our squabbling and the car park plan was approved after all.

In retrospect the story tells us something about the nature of the debate on architecture in the 1960s and 1970s. There was quite simply a taboo about talking about atmosphere, beauty and character. And there is a sense in which this taboo has never been broken.

Atmospheres as a Departure Point

My interest in the background and significance of architecture, and in the question of how we can take the new functionalism further has in fact never ceased to preoccupy me. This fascination has also had a profound influence on my designs and projects of that period – my own two houses, Amsterdam City Hall, Centre Pompidou, Mijnsherenland, the World Trade Center in Rotterdam and Lelystad Town Hall.

The home I designed for myself in around 1960 was based on or inspired by the prehistoric dwellings I came across in the Vesère valley in France. Like these cave dwellings, the space developed like a snail's shell from the swimming pool terraces to the high living room as a semi-private space to the lower sitting room behind the fireplace and ending up in the most secluded space, namely the bedroom.

I repeated this theme in my second house. The high degree of seclusion and the sequence from seclusion to openness are the essential architectural theme here.

This spatial scenario also played a dominant role in the competition design of 1968 for Amsterdam City Hall. A city hall is a complicated spatial system. As a user or visitor you can easily feel lost. I therefore wanted it to emanate a sense of security. The complicated spatial system of the building is therefore clustered round an atrium shaped like an hourglass with its narrowest part at the Dutch reference level (the Amsterdam Ordnance Datum or NAP). Beneath the NAP the atrium expands out-

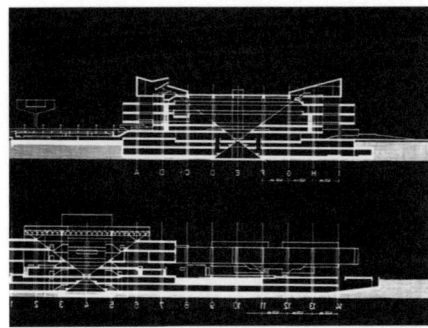

fig. 5.7   City Hall in Amsterdam
(cross section)

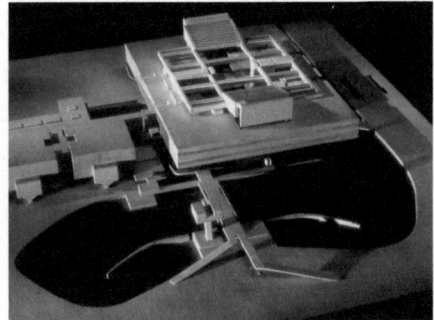

City Hall in Amsterdam   fig. 5.8

wards below, while above the NAP it expands outwards and upwards towards a glass roof covering the whole space. Through the glass roof one can see the stars. Below the NAP the clouds are reflected in reverse in a water surface. This interplay of spaces around the narrowest point creates a camera-obscura effect.

I emphasized the NAP because all measurements of altitude throughout the world are based on it. With the choice of an hourglass as a standard for measuring altitude, I was anticipating the theme of "space – time – movement" that I would later explore in depth.

In fact the design for Amsterdam City Hall was a bid to endow a spatial system with an organizational meaning through differences in measurements and atmosphere. The deliberately planned scenario gives the person experiencing it a pleasant sense of finding his bearings. The building helps one to answer dormant or latent questions such as "where am I?" and "where was I?"

Spatial Experience, Atmosphere and Security

Eloquent spatiality is an important facet of the power of expression of architecture and has always played a role in my designs.

One built example of this sort of spatial work is the design for the Ministry of Housing, Spatial Planning and Environment (VROM) of 1985. What was involved here was the question of how you can give 3,250 civil servants the space they need in a building in such a way that they also feel "at home" there. In this design the additional non-functional space is a more evident presence than the functional working area: there are plenty of atria, voids and built-in balconies. This additional space fulfils a role as emblem of the building.

The VROM building was followed by a series of plans in which the theme of space was dominant. Prior to the design process, the atmosphere was the real issue. Sometimes, as in the case of the VROM building, this led to a series of linked spaces. In other cases, such as the Jungerhans skyscraper in Rotterdam, the result was series of spaces stacked one above another.

How themes such as space, the experience of space, atmosphere and seclusion gradually took on an increasingly purposeful place in my work can be seen in my more recent designs.

In my opinion what was required for the concert hall of the Muziekschool building in Zeist was a sense of intimacy. This is often the first time that students perform in public. They are children who are playing for their family and friends. I therefore rejected the traditional confrontational arrangement of a stage versus serried ranks of seats. The auditorium is designed in such a way that the rows of seats seem to be embracing the musicians on the stage.

The theme of the design for the church in Harderwijk is a stole, the garment worn by priests. This stole forms a boundary for the partially circular liturgical center. The demarcated shape of the liturgical center expands upward inside the lining of the stole into the full circle of the win-

fig. 5.9   VROM, The Hague

Town Hall, Lelystad fig. 5.10

dow in the roof. Light falls from this round window onto a pleated room. A poetic and mystical atmosphere is thus deliberately conjured up. The floor plan is a partial pentagram that forms the basis of the golden section. In this plan spatial effect and presentation are interdependent. During the design process the atmosphere of seclusion and contemplation was the central concern.
The final design is the Music Cluster, a music and theater center in Enschede. It is a typical instance where I, as an architect, had in-depth discussions with the client about which atmosphere to give the interior. We used paintings to structure our conversations. After quite an adventurous quest we settled for two paintings by Gustav Klimt – *The Kiss* and *Water Nymph*. The atmosphere of these paintings was translated into three-dimensional terms in the interiors. *The Kiss* was used for the Opera Foyer and the *Water Nymph* for the Pop Music Foyer.

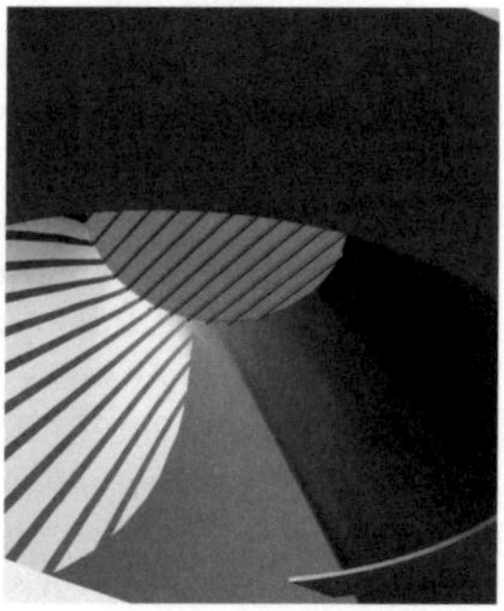

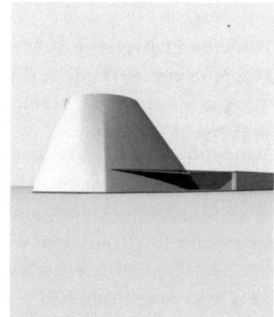

fig. 5.11 Church, in Harderwijk

Good Architecture Conjures up Emotions

When I review my work, it is as clear as daylight that the spatial aspect of architecture has been my preoccupation right from the outset. I realize now that thinking in terms of feelings and atmospheres has always been a factor in my own work. But this mode of thought was always smuggled on board as a sort of stowaway. It never got its rightful place or the recognition it deserves. And as long as that seemingly indescribable thing remains unnamed, it can never gain a fully-fledged place in the prevailing rational process of design and construction. I have thus come to the conclusion that the work of planning the atmosphere of a space must have a guaranteed place, so that the hype and the rational aspects of the process aren't allowed to swamp the proceedings.

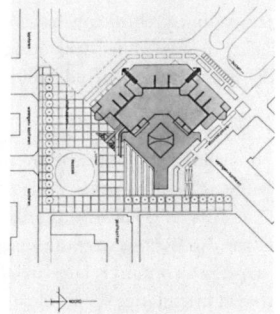

fig. 5.12 Church, in Harderwijk

This brings me back to Sloterdijk. Poetic or atmospheric thought, as he says, produces "spatial creations". Spatial creations are experienced intuitively. They are then manufactured rationally, until finally, as in architecture, they serve as concrete vehicles of the atmosphere intended from the start.
Good architecture conjures up atmospheres and emotions. Experiencing architecture is a matter of intuition. Designing architecture therefore cannot be done without thinking in terms of atmospheres. And again Sloterdijk says: Living in spheres means producing a dimension that humans can comprehend. Spheres are spatial creations that function as immune systems for ecstatic creatures who feel "the outside" act upon themselves.
One might well argue that it is precisely this atmospheric mode of thinking that can not be comprehended and that it is therefore impracticable – but I don't believe that. The American philosopher Martha Nussbaum has said on this subject that an idea is preceded by an image that develops in stages, that in principle it still is multi-interpretable, more an atmosphere then a concrete fact. It is strik-

fig. 5.13 Town Hall, Lelystad

All the visual material in this essay comes from Ector Hoogstad Architecten

ing that Peter Sloterdijk says more or less the same thing, only in different words. He speaks of an "Innenraum Schöpfung die Übertragungsliebe befordert" – the creation of an inner space that stimulates the love of communication.

A sort of mental space is thus generated in our thought, a specific emotion, which is initially indistinct but which gradually develops into a concrete idea. Or a feeling. In other words, an emotion connects life (experiencing or being) with thought. No matter how vague they may appear then, feelings or atmospheres are essential for our thinking and for our being. They feed our ideas. And emotions are serious choices. But it remains difficult to speak about them. The idea that they resist being captured in language is, I think, a major reason why moods, emotions and atmospheres are absent from the agenda of architects.

Towards a Language of Atmospheres

The problem therefore is that up to now such a thing as a conceptual framework for typical architectural atmospheres has hardly existed. In the absence of concepts or a terminology, there is no way of broaching the topic. It is striking that this has proved possible in other arts, as in music for instance. A composer who is commissioned to compose a festive march will undoubtedly go for a four-four time, will probably use C Major as his key – the so-called 'oompah' scale – and will probably choose an Allegro Moderato for his tempo.

Outside the arts too one finds examples of conceptual frameworks for atmospheres. In advertising for instance an extremely concrete manner of atmospheric thinking has long been employed, based on diagrams derived from the theories of the psychologist Alfred Adler.

The diagram enables one to carry out discussions about the strategic market positioning of a brand. The four poles – Pleasure, Mother Earth, Certainty and Power – do not just give structure to the discussion, they offer words and concepts to carry on a content related debate about something that at first glance seems elusive.

Whether or this diagram can be applied in architecture is an interesting issue. In my opinion it ought to be possible to designate the atmospheric and emotional elements in the design process in such a way as to make them discussible, so that they get the place and thus the recognition they merit. If we succeed in this we will be able to free ourselves of what I call the legacy of rationalism. By restoring atmospheres and feelings to architecture we will get buildings in which people will come into their own once again. And I am convinced that in this way we will breathe new life into architecture.

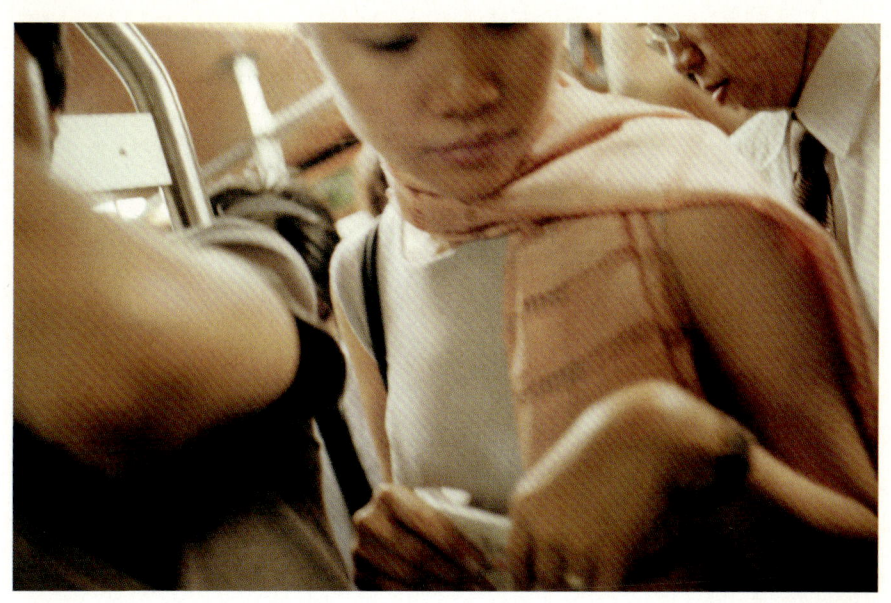

The Condition of Publicity

MARK PIMLOTT

"Societies have always been shaped more by the
nature of the media by which men communicate than
by the content of their communication."
*Marshall McLuhan, The Medium is the Massage:
An Inventory of Effects (1967) New York

ESSAY 06
ARCHITECTURE BULLETIN N° 01|2006

Mark Pimlott (1958) is an artist and architectural designer.
He works in London and The Hague, and currently teaches
architecture at Delft University. Pimlott is seriously concerned about the one-dimensional character architecture tends to assume as architects resort increasingly to
the methods of publicity. In an adaptation of a lecture he
gave in connection with the exhibition Ads & Architects
(NAI, 2005), he cites the work of the so-called avant garde
architects to probe the seductive tactics used in advertising and their implications for our image of architecture.

The past few years have witnessed a notable increase in the
production and projection of architecture that is indebted
to the processes and appearances of publicity. The existence of architecture so oriented is not particularly new. One
can trace a fairly straightforward history of this phenomenon from the latter part of the eighteenth century and the
emergence of the modern public. It becomes a prominent
characteristic of commercial and public architecture, for
example, in the building types of the arcade, the department store and the exhibition building throughout the nineteenth century. The sense that there is now much more
architecture indebted to, dependent upon, and in the thrall
of publicity is in no doubt partly due to the pervasive and
varied nature of contemporary media. The object of architects becoming involved with media seems to turn on its
promise of visibility.

In the mainstream professional setting, publicity has a
rather more pragmatic role to play. Those who have followed the lead of the avant-garde continue to regard pu-
blishing as a viable route to commissions: increased visibility in the architecture and design press is intended to
attract the attention of colleagues and clients. Better still is
exposure in the non-professional arena, such as newspapers

or popular magazines or television features devoted to 'lifestyles.'

The explosion of publicity – in which exposure itself has become more important than that which is exposed – places particular demands on those with special ambitions. It is necessary that such architects pursue both new outlets and new means for the dissemination of their work. These new outlets demand different sorts of presentation: each medium, each outlet has its own specific character, its own tropes its own audience, its own modes of address.

effects. These are difficult requirements for architecture, which carries its own specific history and discourse. Yet, for architecture to communicate in the realm of mass media, these internal 'anachronistic' characteristics have to appear to be either mythologized or subdued, even abandoned.

This is all consistent with a process of simplification for the purpose of access to mass media. Mass media is interested in material as a kind of fodder, which always must be present for the continuing existence of the media.

Normative effects

To become visible in the outlets of the media, the producer has to submit himself to its norms, practices and demands. The press release, for example, is ideally a completely digested version of what an audience must receive to achieve maximum effect. For each media outlet, there is a precise idea of what characterizes its audience. The material to be projected at its audience is tailored for consumption, so that the material 'fits' its expectations. The media outlet responds to and feeds the audience's desire. The audience must be constantly stimulated; everything must be equally tantalizing. If the entry of architecture (not a mainstream subject) into the mainstream of publicity in order to reach a mass audience (hundreds of thousands as opposed to thousands, for example) is to be realized, then the effects upon its presentation, display and conception will be profound. The first transformation that architecture must undergo is a shift towards representation. The architectural project must become a picture of itself: Within a publicity context it must conform to its normative

Promotion

The idea of publicity is to attract attention to a product so that it may be consumed. This is either by a direct sale strategy or an indirect one of association. For example, in a glossy magazine like Vogue a series of associations are generated linking a complex of material together. Adverts, features and editorial content are all related in such a way that they work together. Although each, strictly, has a different format or appearance, each defers to its associate; each promotes and so constitutes a kind of product. All of these products are both adjacent and interwoven, configured to complete a complex that is the media platform. From this platform, 'products' are registered and accepted by readers because of their associations with other 'products.' Each element of the media platform works in concert with the other, each is in a kind of agreement with the other: what does not fit is assigned to the periphery, publicity's blind spot. Publicity works through a variety of expressions in one direction.

That one direction characterizes the relationship between the media platform and the public — the audience — attracted to its package. The audience is restrained, restricted to the role of the consumer. The media platform exists to be the outlet for its sponsors, who are visible through advertising and promoted through 'features.' The media platform simultaneously conceals and reveals a political-economic dimension shaped by its sponsors, reflecting their value system. The value system is the message inadvertently consumed by its audience.

The consumer is tied to a one-way contract, entangled in an environment constituted by an array of products that must be associated with, desired and consumed. In this relationship, the consumer is manipulated into an agreement whose terms are dictated by the media platform. Yet it is presented as a tacit agreement between the media platform and its 'audience.' The public is reduced to the condition of a consumer, whose responses are limited to those that are predetermined. It is the logical evolution of what is always implied by the "Consumers' Republic." *Lisbeth Cohen, Is There an Urban History of Consumption?, p. 91

The Medium is the Massage

"The medium, or process, of our time is reshaping and restructuring patterns of social interdependence and every aspect of our personal life. It is forcing us to reconsider and re-evaluate practically every thought, every action, and every institution formerly taken for granted. Everything is changing — you, your family, your neighborhood, your education, your job, your government, your relation to 'the others'."
*Marshall McLuhan, The Medium is the Massage

The media platform is, itself, a medium. The medium can either aspire to the condition of reality, which necessitates its transparency and hence, its own invisibility; or it can recognize its own artifice. Artifice is a veil that promises, but never delivers, fulfillment, necessary to the production of desire.

At present, media (advertising, publicity and their vehicles — newspapers, magazines, television, mainstream cinema, mail-shots, internet) seem to indulge in exaggerated artificiality, partly because it can be technically achieved, and partly because it constitutes such a profound departure from the everyday. This artificiality is characterized by an extensive, fetishized, synthetic surface. The surface is paramount, the agent of a seduction realized through movement, detail, abundance, repetition and allusion. All known imagery can be called upon to contribute to the surface's attributes. The surface is sophisticated, keened to the conditions of its contexts, the scenes of its visibility. This sophistication is honed through the combined efforts of executives, market researchers, publicists, advertising agency's art directors and copywriters, production art directors and technicians, modelling agencies, casting directors, stylists, make-up artists, photographers and post-production art directors and editors, and public relations specialists. The crafted surface that results is extremely artificial: a complete representation. The surface has an irresistible aura.

In the case of publicity, representation has a specific purpose, which is to direct the viewer or the consumer to agree to its fantasy. This constitutes the commencement of an agreement to terms, beginning with the association of the representation with the product, and consummated with the act of consuming. The deep stereotyping that is involved in the crafting of auratic surfaces, the inter-relationships between these surfaces and their supports and contexts, and the extensions of these networks into the public world, is malignant and corrosive. Publicity shapes society to conform to predictable patterns of consumption.

The commercial break

In American advertisements seen in the pages of magazines or broadcast on television after the Second World War, the environ-ment of representation devised for the typical, nuclear American family simply seemed to be re-presented; contemporary magazine spreads and television screens were both offered as and taken to be 'windows on the world.' These representations assumed the mantle of transparency: they made a play to their audience (for the period between 1945 and 1968 projected as and conceived of as relatively homogeneous) to not be representations at all. They purported, instead, to be truth.

In the making of an advertisement, much effort is made in getting all elements and aspects of the scene to be consistent in their illuminated portrayal of their subject, which or who serves as the support, the vehicle for a particular product or service. All that appears is laden with meaning, with significance that is legible on conscious and unconscious levels to the viewer or the consumer.

The viewer is asked to recognize the protagonists of the advertisement, and then to identify with them: either as reflections of themselves, or as role models for the kinds of people they think they ought to be.

American examples of the 1950s and 1960s are not obsolete. They demonstrate that publicity and its projected environment – the condition of publicity – is political by nature, wherein relationships are established or reinforced between certain people in society while others are discouraged; relationships are defined and instituted between producers and consumers; and 'desirable' relationships are described between people and authority.

Publicity's efforts to shape responses to products to induce the desire to consume remain undimmed, even refreshingly old-fashioned, despite their increased diversity and responsiveness to new audiences, markets and niches.

Celebrity

Herein lies the attraction for today's architect: architecture is another feature of the world of couture, commodity and celebrity. An increasingly common tendency sees buildings described by images that prioritize its abstract properties; by one-line descriptions in the form of sound-bites, whose internal organizations can be described by a series of stacked words whose size reflect their projected dimensions; as branding.

Architecture that does the work of branding generates Louis Vuitton buildings that look like Louis Vuitton products, or signature architecture by designer-authors. It generates an architecture of image made to be taken as the real thing, in the manner of a Venturi 'duck.' *Robert Venturi; Denise Scott Brown; Steven Izenour Learning from Las Vegas It advocates abuses of representation. Consistent with this trope is Daniel Libeskind's proposition that a building that resembles a fragmented globe should be considered a symbol of a shattered world, and therefore says: 'war museum.' The mawkish publicity that accompanies such productions indulges and endorses such banalities.

Publicity and architecture

Publicity offers a particular kind of relationship between architecture and its public, which it treats as its audience. Through its address, it establishes a distance that can only be bridged by consumption. This is a one-way contract, whose terms must be accepted in toto: no re-interpretation is on offer. In architecture, it means a product for a market of consumers: addressed as individuals but regarded as a mass bound by measured desires and averaged means. This is quite different from an architecture made for a real public, a society. The 'market' is frequently championed by monetarists as the true representation of human interests. Yet that same market is hostile to the idea of society if it means collections of people who associate unpredictably. It is opposed to the public, the civic.

The political aspect of this is self-evident: in order to consume, one has to accept what is on offer and choose. The public is rendered passive. This gives the producer power: it makes the producer a player, whose interests consequently assume undue importance, requiring protection by government legislation, influencing the form of the State.

Conforming to the conditions of consumption diminishes the nature of the architectural commission, architecture, the architect, and finally, the relation between the public and the built project, the city and society. If the idea of the architect playing to such a market is questionable, why does the so-called avant-garde participate in such tactics? While certainly self-serving, there is something essentially conservative about the avant-garde's rush to commodification. Even its critique, or rhetoric posing as critique, is obliged to conform to publicity's conditions, and the order of relations with an audience that publicity demands. An example is Rem Koolhaas's S, M, L, XL, and its back cover 'press release' in praise of itself.

Architecture that accepts the conditions of publicity addresses the public as consumers, whose desires it anticipates, preconditions and predetermines. The work that accepts the conditions of publicity agrees to its terms and ideology. It can be sophisticated, knowing, ironic, aware of its context – it can communicate – but it cannot allow the possibility of interpretation. Interpretation is not the same as 'interaction,' which is offered as a sop to the consumer's 'individuality,' and is merely another interface for pre-determined responses.

Surfaces, appropriations and the avant-garde

The generation of unique ideas and artefacts is concomitant with the avant-garde. Its effort is obliged to be exceptional, specific, unique, culturally distinct from the production that surrounds it; as distinct from mainstream cultural production as that production is distinct from the unconscious world. Within the cultural setting, the work (if legitimize) assumes value through its originality.

As the work of the avant-garde aspires to the condition of publicity, it enters the mechanisms and values of the market, wherein its uniqueness is translated into value. The work becomes associated with other luxury commodities. The work is obliged to behave in much the same way as other luxury items, which, though mass-produced, bear the fictions of their uniqueness, their unrepeatability.

The most successful self-styled avant-garde architectural practices and the institutions that legitimize them have recognized the authority of the market and the necessity of tying their fortunes to it. Institutions and producers have accordingly marketed themselves to comply with publicity's requirements and processes. In publicity, all subjects are 'sold,' treated as commodities, requiring publicity. The logic of the marketing of the luxury item (and hence architecture) is that it must express its enhanced value to as broad an audience as possible. It demands widespread publicity across different media outlets, each addressing specific audience profiles. Effective communication across media and people tends to prioritize forms of address, flattening and simplifying the subject of publicity in the process, reinforcing its surface.

There are a multitude of outlets where publicity might make its appearance. Despite their particularities, these presentations take on typical forms that follow from supplied imagery, the press release and the biography — factual or fictional — of the 'author.' The imagery must be both durable and flexible because of its repeated presentation. The repetition itself makes claims for the legitimacy of artefact and author. When one turns to contemporary architects, only a few have come through the media filter: Koolhaas, Hadid, Gehry, Libeskind, Starck, Herzog (so many others hope to be amongst them). Their production is iconic and hence familiar; so are their faces, which appear in publicity as frequently as the buildings and interiors they design.

The mediated, fetishized image of the luxury item offers a surface that stands in for its actual counterpart. Replacing the artefact, the representation is taken to be the artefact. The artefact becomes a token of its own representation, confirming its represented surface as real. Publicity creates a similar condition for the work of architecture. The mediated version of the architecture/ text/ author acts as a substitute for the architecture; the built architecture is taken as congruous with the publicity that surrounds it and makes it visible, rendering its actuality redundant. There is no true congruity, of course: buildings exist in the world, with actual characteristics, physicality, and spaces. But they also exist as their mediated images; as products of their authors; as objects in the space of culture and commodities and gossip and personality: their mediated existences — their condition within publicity — affect their nature in the actual, physical world.

What is taken to be an obligation to publicity — particularly by the avant-garde — affects not only architecture's presentation, but architecture itself, its forms, and the relations to and between people that it projects. Architecture (inadvertently or not) acts as an agent of interests' ideologies other than its own. The association of architecture with commodity-value, particularly the commodities related to 'cultural production,' directs it towards the condition of those commodities. Assuming characteristics germane to them, architecture confuses itself with fashion and contemporary art and vice versa. In the fumbling that emerges from their facile confusion, primacy is given to surface, encouraged by the placidly anti-critical environment of publicity.

In such an environment, the producer is regarded and regards himself as a celebrity, producing baubles for the adornment of his Ego and the World. His projections become spectacles in a system of entertainment, where amusement is a substitute for engagement, a contemporary panem et cirsenses. The viewer or the citizen surrenders his status, reduced to a paying customer before spectacles undimmed by either his presence or absence.

REFERENCES

- Cohen, L., Is there an urban history of consumption?, In: Journal of Urban History, 29:2, 2003, p. 87-106.
- Mc Luhan, M., The Medium is the Massage; An Inventory of Effects, New York, Bantam, 1967.
- Venturi, R., Izenour, S. en D. Scott Brown, Learning from Las Vegas, Cambridge, Mass. The MIT Press, 1972.

The Rotterdam City Hall Models

Architectural Models as an Expression of Civic Pride?

ELLEN SMIT

ESSAY 07

ARCHITECTURE BULLETIN N° 01|2006

Ellen Smit (1965) is an architectural historian, and has worked as a curator in the NAI's Collection Department since 2001. She specializes in the architecture and planning of the twentieth century, and is currently project leader for the acquisition of the Rotterdam City Hall models. "In our society which is so strongly influenced by visual culture, we seem to have become incapable of forming a conception of architecture without the help of a two-dimensional image. Architects who give lectures without accompanying PowerPoint presentations or slide shows are no longer to be found. So it is all the more remarkable that the same discussion took place a hundred years ago, although in a radically different way. Suspicions about the potential manipulation of images had reached such a pitch that architectural models were preferred to drawings."

The Netherlands Architecture Institute is currently home to some twenty architectural models of Rotterdam's City Hall (1910-1920) on Coolsingel. They consist of four competition models and sixteen detail models of the design that was eventually built, the one by architect, professor and historian Henri Evers (1855-1929). Not only are the models tangible, three-dimensional links with the past which emanate a powerful historical sensation, they throw also new light on several aspects of Dutch architectural history.

This essay will argue that the models are susceptible to interpretation as specific expressions of a civic culture in Rotterdam, at a juncture when representative, monumental architecture saw its first opportunity to reappear in the city after decades in the sway of engineering pragmatism. The extremely high level of detail and the large dimensions of the models are due to the specific intentions of the Rotterdam city government to symbolize the prosperity of Rotterdam by means of an urban project of monumental beauty.

It is also clear that the models are a valuable document of how architectural design was practiced in around 1913. In particular, they yield interesting information about the functional relationship between architectural models and drawings. Moreover, the models form part of a long tradition of working in plaster of Paris, and they reveal a relation between the possibilities of the material and the visualization of a monumental architectural style.

CULTURAL PLURALISM

Despite the imminence of war in 1913, the year when the competition for the new Rotterdam City Hall took place, the Netherlands was flushed with a sense of optimism, a feeling of standing on the threshold of a new world. The year 1913, named the Jubilee Year, would see both the centenary of the Netherlands as an independent monarchy, and the World Peace Congress taking place in The Hague. The cultural climate was full of self-confidence, as was apparent from the numerous events and exhibitions displaying the best the Netherlands had to offer in the areas of art, culture, trade, industry and shipping. The main tradition in architecture, the "mother of the arts", was that of the École de Beaux-Arts, a design methodology that combined prototypical rectangular and square plans with monumental modeling and structural innovations. But much was possible in artistic and stylistic respects, for the approach was not governed by a normative ideal of beauty. Progressive tendencies such as Art Deco, Orientalism, the Amsterdam School and Functionalism had already left their mark. But a luxuriant historicism still flourished, with tradition and novelty layered one over the other, without either wholly dominating. Thus a wide diversity of styles and movements burgeoned in both architecture and fine art.

ARTISTIC SYNTHESIS

The competition for the Rotterdam City Hall on Coolsingel is a splendid illustration of the growing self-confidence of a city bent on raising its cultural and aesthetic profile. Henri Evers's implemented design was one of the most characteristic examples in the Netherlands of prestige architecture modeled on the French Beaux-Arts school. With its symmetrical ground plan, French Renaissance style structure, Dutch Renaissance stepped gables, Oriental central plan and other ingredients in Egyptian, Byzantine, Romanesque and Gothic styles, the building was Dutch Eclecticism at its apogee. The architect, professor and historian Henri Evers and the city architect A. J. Th. Kok designed the building down to the last interior details. At both concrete and abstract levels, the building is an architectural Gesamtkunstwerk. In concrete respects, architecture operated as the "mother of the arts", whose custody gave a meaningful context to the arts of mural painting, sculpture and stained glass. From an abstract point of view, the city hall was to be a public symbol of the vigor, growth and importance of Rotterdam; and to achieve this, artists from a variety of disciplines, such as the painter Johan Thorn Prikker, the sculptor Simon Miedema and the stained-glass artist Henricus worked under the leadership of Evers and Kok to substantiate an iconographic program in praise of Rotterdam as a world-class port and city of industry.

"O LEELIJK, LEELIJK, LEELIJK ZIJT GIJ, INDUSTRIEEL NIEUW ROTTERDAM"

O ugly, ugly, ugly art thou, industrial new Rotterdam; these were the words of the author and poet E.J. Potgieter (1808-1875) after he visited the city in the latter years of his life. His reproach was not just from a cursory impression, but was a weighty judgement which remained unshaken for decades. Potgieter was referring here to the lopsided development of the Rotterdam harbor and industry. No other city in the Netherlands grew as explosively as Rotterdam in the period from 1850 to 1900. The digging of a shipping canal called the Nieuwe Waterweg ushered in a period of expansion of the docks, flourishing commerce and a surge in population from one hundred and sixteen thousand to over four hundred thousand souls. The city first betrayed its metropolitan ambitions with huge urban expansion schemes in western and southern directions, and the development of a commercial center on the margins of the existing triangular inner city. The city's planning was dominated by improvements to the docks and the system of waterways, and to the construction of new housing districts for workers and their families. Two city architect/civil engineers of the nineteenth century, W.N. Rose (1801-1877) and G.J. de Jong (1845-1917) had already given Rotterdam a rigorous facelift. Rose's "Waterproject" fed fresh water from the River Maas into the city's canals thereby helping improve the health standard of Rotterdam's inhabitants. The uncompromising approach of De Jong, the director of the Municipal Works Department, resulted in the combination of modern harbor expansion schemes with a thrifty and pragmatic housing development policy. New harbors and housing estates proliferated rapidly on the south bank of the Maas, while the private owners had a complete say over how development would take place. Without the restraint of an integrated town planning strategy, the result was wholly lacking in urban aesthetics.

IDENTITY UNDER ATTACK

A.R. Zimmerman (1869-1939) appeared on the scene as the new, ambitious mayor of Rotterdam in 1906. He had relinquished his post as the mayor of Dordrecht for this purpose and, at the age of 37, he must have felt the appointment to the much larger city of Rotterdam as a major promotion. Zimmerman was widely-traveled man with many international contacts, and his horizons extended farther than the borders of the Netherlands.

What kind of city did Zimmerman take over? It was a city where Potgieter's words still rang true and where monumental civic architecture was no more than a sporadic feature of the townscape. It was a city that had too little to offer its wealthy and prominent citizens, on whom the green villa parks of other towns in the region such as Voorburg and Wassenaar exerted an irresistible attraction. It was a city that lacked the urban green space for those same citizens to enjoy a refreshing Sunday walk. And, above all, it was a city whose core identity was under attack.

The construction of an elevated railway in 1874 had necessitated the filling-in of a city-center canal, the Blaak; the result was to create a visual schism in the historic city center, splitting it in two. The elevated railway also resulted in the building of a new railway station on the west of the inner city, thus sparking off the growth of Rotterdam in the area around Coolvest and Hofplein. This development gave the locality an ambiguous character, eliminating the historic functions of the city wall and the city entrance. Their physical outlines still remained, however: the moat still contained water, and a city gateway and two windmills survived as relics of bygone times. On one side of Coolvest, the west, the grander scale of city planning announced itself with the construction of the new Coolsingel Hospital (designed by Rose) and the Tivoli Theater. The opposite side, where the inner city fabric of narrow streets and alleys still prevailed, included the Zandstraat neighborhood, a colorful locality much frequented by sailors with countless bars and brothels and a popular mentality of "live and let live".

RESPECTABLE SOCIETY ATTACKS

Zimmerman saw it as his clear duty to rehabilitate the inner city of Rotterdam. He placed the building of a new city hall in a wider perspective: spurred on by admiration for the urban renovations of Paris and Brussels, he proposed filling in Coolvest, the moat forming the western boundary of the historic city, to create a metropolitan boulevard all the way from Hofplein to Van Hogendorpsplein. He also made provision for the widening of Meent, a street which crossed Coolsingel at right angles, in order to link the new boulevard with the east and west of the city. With this plan, Zimmerman would not only create a new city center with Coolsingel as its main traffic artery, but would also eradicate the small-scale and, in his view, moribund neighborhoods along Coolvest. The cramped houses and impoverished residents of Zandstraat and the adjoining streets would be swept aside for his vision of the future: a new city hall and a new main post office, inspired by a blend of Beaux Arts and the City Beautiful, whose grand scale and exuberance of ornament and symbolism would grace the inner city of Rotterdam; a new center worthy of Rotterdam as a world metropolis.

INNER CIRCLE

The municipal government of Rotterdam had long consisted of prominent representatives of trade, industry and the arts, whose social eminence seemingly entitled them to call the shots in their city. Zimmerman, who has gone down in history as an authoritarian mayor, was thus encircled by municipal councilors whose outlook on society and city government scarcely differed from his own. In his pursuit of a beautiful city, Zimmerman gathered an inner circle of like minded citizens around him, consisting of Evers as well as J. Verheul Dzn and P.G. Buskens, both architects as well as city councillors. Evers himself was firmly embedded in Rotterdam's cultural and political scene. He had been the head of the architecture department of the Rotterdam Academy of Fine Arts since 1887 and had designed among the Remonstrantse Kerk on Westersingel (1895), as well as, the Caland Monumument on Van Hogendorpsplein (1906), which was commissioned

fig. 7.1 Scale model of the design with the motto Green and White of Jan Stuyt

fig. 7.2 Scale model of the design with the motto Rotterdami Prosperitas of Alb.Otten and W.F Overeijnder

fig. 7.3 Scale model of the design with the motto Representative of W.Kromhout Czn.

by Zimmerman's predecessor as mayor, s'Jacob. Evers was a man of high standing, who combined intellectual distinction with a cosmopolitan life-style occasioned by his architectural activities in Antwerp, Brussels, Vienna and Budapest. He had a small oeuvre as a building architect but carried considerable weight as a theorist. With his profes-sorial chair at the Delft University of Technology (1902-1926), Evers held the most sought-after po-sition in Dutch architectural education. His views on architecture and ideas about aesthetics were founded on a knowledge and appreciation of the history of architecture, and underlay the publica-tion of "De architectuur in hare hooftijdperken" ("The Main Ages of Architecture", 1901). This book was received with immediate enthusiasm, went through several reprints, and was used as a text-book at the Academies of Architecture and at Delft University. Evers's book presented a meticu-lous account of the characteristics, proportions and harmonic concepts of various architectural styles such as the Gothic and the Renaissance. In his own work, he aspired to the lasting beauty and permanent values of architecture. He championed an aesthetics of building which rose above ephem-eral fashions and whims, and which could only come about through deep insight into the essence of historical architectural styles.

The intercession of Evers led in 1902 to the ap-pointment of the architect Verheul to member-ship of the Rotterdam City Council. Evers recom-mended Verheul to the councilors on account of his technical and artistic proficiency. As a council-lor, Verheul strove to preserve the beauty of his-toric Rotterdam while developing it into a city of international allure that would still be a pleasant place to live. He fought for the conservation of historically significant buildings and for carefully considered action in urban development, both for expansions and the inner city. Verheul's ideal picture of Rotterdam was closely bound up with the city's beauty in its glory days of the eighteenth century, as a trading city with imposing merchants' houses. In Verheul's view, the "remorseless" nine-teenth century had brought mainly disfigurement of the existing civic fabric. He thought the grand boulevards and squares of Brussels and Paris of-fered appropriate examples for a new, prestigious civic core in Rotterdam.

THE ROTTERDAM CITY HALL COMPETITION

Zimmerman, Buskens and Verheul had already prepared situation plans for the new Rotterdam City Hall before the competition was announced. The projecting corner pavilions and the central ressault were already present in concept. Zim-merman then asked Evers to create a preliminary design for the city hall and a development plan for the new Coolsingel boulevard.

After Evers submitted his preliminary design, the council assented nonetheless to a proposal from the city hall committee to hold a limited competi-tion. The invited designers were H. Evers, K.P.C. de Bazel, W. Kromhout, J. Stuyt, C.B. van der Tak, M. Brinkman and the team of A. Otten and W.F. Over-eijnder. The competition brief was accompanied by two ground plans of the preliminary design drawn by Evers. The brief stated that the ground plans were not binding for the participants, but were in-tended only to clarify the possibilities of building on the available site. The designers were entirely free as regards architectural style, but had to main-tain a clear distinction between the prestigious public section of the city hall, which must lie on Coolsingel, and the administrative functions to be accommodated at the rear. Besides the customary functions for a city hall (the council chamber, mar-riage halls, a banqueting hall and offices) the brief explicitly listed a monumental main staircase, a capacious vestibule and a statue of Johan van Ol-debarneveld among its formal requirements.

COMPETITION MODELS AND
PERSPECTIVE DRAWINGS

The competition participants were instructed to visualize their designs largely in the form of black-and-white drawings. They were not required to submit colored perspectives, as some architectur-al competitions did in that period. To give an im-pression of the visual qualities of the exterior, the brief instead asked for the submission of a colored model at 1:50 scale, with the facade on Coolsingel and the two side elevations elaborated in detail.

The competition models which were submitted were both monumental in character and meticulously executed, all devoting meticulous attention to the architectural detailing of arches, capitals, moldings, cornices and ornaments, and to the representation of materials and colors. Apart from that of Jan Stuyt, all the models were made in plaster of Paris, which was much used for that purpose in the period. Centuries of experience in the use of plaster and the techniques for processing it (molding, casting, detailed carving and painting) made it an ideal material for representing monumental historicist architecture. The purpose of the competition models was to convey the intended final architectural image. From the viewpoint of the designer, the model needed to make a powerful aesthetic impression in order to convince the jury and the city councillors of the beauty of the design and so to qualify for the first prize.

It is noteworthy that the competition specifically called for the submission of colored models rather than colored perspective drawings, which would obviously have been less arduous and hence less expensive to prepare. There had been a wave of criticism around 1900 questioning the value of perspective drawings as a credible medium of communication. The immediate cause was the allegedly misleading character of the perspective drawings sent in for the Stock Exchange competition in Amsterdam (1885). These views represented the extremely long elevation on Damrak in a highly foreshortened and hence misleading way. A scale model, it was held, was not amenable to the same kind of optical deception, since there was no possibility of elongating or shortening elevations and towers at will. The substitution of models for perspective drawings was connected to a debate that was not confined to the Netherlands: in 1900, the Royal Institute of British Architects had forbidden the submission of perspective drawings to competitions.

Hence the competition models for Rotterdam City Hall had a prominent place in the architect's communication with the client: the models were not just an adjunct to the drawings, but replace the perspective views. The city hall models differed in this respect from those submitted to the competition for the Peace Palace in The Hague (1905). There, the competition rules requested colored perspective drawings and models were not required. However, some architects including H.P. Berlage and Ed. Cuypers did submit them. The models concerned were uncolored, being executed in untreated clay or white-painted plaster of Paris. Their purpose was in this instance solely to give an impression of the building mass and the disposition of turrets and domes, and they did not attempt to reflect the pictorial quality and architectural detailing of the design.

The drawings and model Berlage made for his first design of the Gemeentemuseum in The Hague (1919-1920) are similarly interrelated. Berlage prepared brightly colored perspective drawings of his design, which visualizes its atmosphere, colors and architectural detailing. The white plaster model functioned as an adjunct to the drawings and illustrated the intended composition of architectural volumes.

COMPETITION MODELS AS EXPRESSIONS OF STYLE

The Rotterdam City Hall competition models present only the exterior of the building and reveal nothing about how the designs are organized

fig. 7.4 Scale model of the design with the motto Pro Domo Sua of C.B. van der Tak

fig. 7.5 Scale model of the design with the motto Aquarius of K.P.C. de Bazel

fig. 7.6 Scale model of the design with the motto J.J. of M. Brinkman

internally. This shows that they were intended to convey only the exterior appearance and not the plan or distribution of spaces. The plans of all the entries remained firmly within the Beaux-Arts tradition. They are derived from that system's prototype plans, which are rectangular or square and have a system of courtyards and axes. The arrangement of spaces played scarcely any part in the deliberations of the competition jury, since they could rely on it conforming to the renowned and familiar pattern. There was no unequivocal benchmark for the exterior style, however. By 1913 the dominant academic classicism and the dogmatic revival styles had been replaced by a pluralist eclecticism blended with more novel artistic traits. The seven models for Rotterdam City Hall show how the architects sought inspiration in the past, but also tried to devise a new form of city hall to represent a prosperous city on the threshold of a new era. In modern Rotterdam, the city hall needed to be an artistic synthesis, a building whose applied style and decorative program would make it significant to the present and the future alike. All the designs were committed to mining the stylistic riches of the past, but they combined this with efforts to make a design that reflected the dawn of a new age. Quotations from the Italian and French Renaissance, the Gothic and more novel styles such as Art Nouveau and Orientalism all appear in the models, but in their quest for a new style and a new urban culture, the architects displayed a liberal, individual creativity in their architectural ideas which was characteristic of the cultural climate in 1913. It is precisely this liberty with the past that makes the designs for Rotterdam City Hall so interesting. This is what places them precisely on the incipient rift with the past that was to become definitive in the years that followed, with the breakthrough of the Amsterdam School, De Stijl, Wendingen and subsequently Modernism.

Furthermore, the designs are convincing antecedents of the postmodern architecture which was to start appearing around 1970. The models testify not to a prevailing, fixed aesthetic but rather to an individualist, proto-postmodern attitude. In this respect they cast a different, more relative, light on what is held to be the revolutionary breakthrough of postmodern architecture in the 1970s.

EVERS'S DESIGN IN THREE DIMENSIONS

In their evaluation of the submitted designs, the City Hall jury considered none of them suitable for execution. The jury did agree however that the entries by H. Evers, J. Stuyt and K.P.C. de Bazel were worthy of the first, second and third prizes respectively. They proposed either choosing between the designs of Evers and Stuyt, or asking both of them to submit a second, improved draft design. Zimmerman, as the chairman of both the City Hall Committee and of the jury, placed his own personal stamp on the jury report. He managed to edit it and the recommendations of the City Hall Committee so creatively that only the recommendation to execute Evers's design was eventually placed before the city council. On 5 June 1913, Rotterdam City Council accordingly voted to build the city hall according to the design by Henri Evers.

Evers elaborated his initial design in the course of 1913, and his drawings were regularly discussed at meetings of the City Hall Committee. After a about a year of this process, the committee began to express criticism of Evers's design and of the progress being made. They were dissatisfied with the aesthetic quality and the way the design was drawn. Evers was repeatedly required to prepare new drawings, of the tower for example. He himself admitted that due to his activities as a professor at Delft he had grown out of touch with architectural practice and no longer possessed the knowledge and expertise needed to function as the chief architect of the city hall. With his consent, the city architect A.J.Th. Kok was appointed to assist Evers in the design work. Shortly after this decision, in 1914, Evers and Kok proposed commissioning a model maker to prepare detailed models of various sections of the building such as the public hall, the tower, the central hall, the front facade and the exterior of the council chamber. The models were probably prepared by the sculptor Hermanus Schellenberg, whom Evers may well have known from his days as a lecturer at the academy in Rotterdam.

The detailed models of Evers's design for Rotterdam City Hall form an extensive and highly detailed series. Several of them, such as those of roofs and domes, were probably instructional models made to aid the masons and decorators during construction. Most of them, however, were unmistakably designed for their aesthetic impact. They represent parts of the design, such as the public hall, the council chamber and sections of the front elevations, with considerable accuracy and detail. It is remarkable that certain sections such as the entrance and the exterior of the mayor's office were visualized in the same way in a number of models at a highly detailed scale (1:10 and 1:20). Since the preparation of models of this kind was a time-consuming and expensive business, it remains puzzling that Rotterdam City Council decided to have them made. They can hardly have served as an amplification of Evers's supposedly "deficient" drawings, since the sculptor could only have made the models on the basis of the architect's drawings. The models would obviously have served to inform the City Hall Committee about the intended design, yet they go well beyond that pragmatic function. The detailed models of Evers's design thank their existence to a confident, ambitious city administration determined to showcase the aesthetic enhancement of Rotterdam with unrestrained exuberance.

EXHIBITION

The models and drawing of the Rotterdam City Hall competition have been exhibited on several occasions. The competition models were first presented only to the jury and the members of the city council, but later, once the winner had been announced, they were placed on view to the general public. The detail models were exhibited in the site shed (the "models room") on Coolsingel. After completion of the city hall in 1921, an exhibition of the plaster sculptures and models prepared for the construction was held in the attic of the new building.

In all the exhibitions, the models were supported on tall tables. The use of these tables, which were clad in jute down to floor level, was a tradition originating from world exhibitions at which countries displayed crowning achievements in art, industry and architecture. Placing the models at this height made them all the more impressive. The viewer was made to feel small and obliged to look up to the facade of the design as though viewing the real building from the street, and thus be deeply impressed by this monumental civic palace and seat of local government. Exhibition of the city hall models in this way testifies once again to the pride of a city council keen to create a monumental, prestigious cityscape in the renewed center of Rotterdam. The Rotterdam City Hall models are convincing evidence of the middle-class offensive Mayor Zimmerman and his inner circle chose to wage.

AFFLUENT CITY

After 1945, during the reconstruction of Rotterdam after the Second Worlds War, the city hall at last laid claim to the urban space that was its due. Its orientation parallel to Coolsingel had hitherto made it impossible for a anyone to view it frontally and so experience its full monumentality. The bombardment of Rotterdam in 1940 opened up new opportunities for urban design, however, particularly since the west side of Coolsingel had taken heavy damage.

The rebuilding of Rotterdam was seen as the restoration of an affluent city with ample space for transport and the nascent consumer society. With construction of the new Lijnbaan shopping street (1949-1953), the architects of the reconstruction plan combined a postwar retail facility with a mon-

fig. 7.7 Scale model of the design with the motto S.P.Q.R of Professor H. Evers

umental view of the city hall. The Korte Lijnbaan street lay on the axis of the city hall and emerged onto a pedestrian plaza, from where the postwar shopping public would be able to enjoy at last the prestigious civic beauty conceived in the twenties.

REFERENCES

– Rotterdam City Archives, archive of the City Hall Building Committee (access no. 408)
– "De prijsvraag voor het Rotterdamsche Raadhuis", Bouwkunst tweemaandelijks tijdschrift gewijd aan de aesthetische, kunsthistorische en technische studie der oude en nieuwe bouwkunst en aanverwante kunstnijverheid vakken, 1913, pp. 89–170.
– R.W. Tieskens et al., Het kleine bouwen : vier eeuwen maquettes in Nederland, exhib. cat. Zutphen 1983
– H. Timmer, Henri Evers 1855-1929 : architect, geschiedschrijver, hoogleraar, BONAS series, Rotterdam, 1997
– A. van der Woud, Waarheid en karakter het debat over de bouwkunst 1840-1900, Rotterdam, NAIPublishers, 1997
– J. de Vries et al., Nederland 1913 een reconstructie van het culturele leven, Amsterdam, Meulenhof/ Landshoff, 1988
– M. Halbertsma, En maar altoos duurt het vitten op het nieuwe raadhuis voort.... het Rotterdamse stadhuis als representatie van Rotterdam 1912–1929, Zwolle, Waanders; Rotterdam, Stichting Kunstprodukties, 1999
– P. van der Laar, Stad van formaat geschiedenis van Rotterdam in de negentiende en twintigste eeuw, Zwolle, Waanders, 1999
– J. Bank, M. van Buuren, 1900 Hoogtij van burgerlijke cultuur Nederlandse Cultuur in Europese context, The Hague, SDU Uitgevers, 2000
– W. Arts, De opkomst en de ondergang van het gips. Een onderzoek naar gipsen maquettes uit de periode 1900-1930, research report for internship NAI/RUG, Rotterdam, 2005

A newer New Orleans

What is to be done?

AARON BETSKY

ESSAY 08

ARCHITECTURE BULLETIN Nº 01 | 2006

Faced with the overwhelming devastation of New Orleans, architects, urban planners, and civil engineers around the world have for months now been asking themselves that obvious question – and others implied by this confrontation between man-made form and nature. Can the art of building solve problems created not by nature alone but by the very ways in which we have historically tried to conquer its potent forces? And on a more practical level, can architecture provide structures that are more logical, just, and useful than those now seemingly ordained by the economic and political powers that be (and not just in the Big Easy)? These, at any rate, were the questions we asked ourselves as the possible contours of a rebuilt New Orleans began to emerge from the destruction wrought by Hurricane Katrina. The situation in New Orleans, it seemed to us, was only an extreme instance of the quandary in which architecture in general finds itself. When the economic "realities" imposed on us by relentless market forces compel the proliferation of nonplaces leached of any individual or social meaning or coherence, how is architecture to respond? When the aim of building is merely to achieve the highest possible return on the smallest possible investment in the shortest amount of time, and when the very notion that urban development should be anchored by common services and communal spaces has all but disappeared, there seems little for architecture to do beyond slapping up prefab high-rises, cloning glass-and-steel office towers, and providing basic shelter for the masses (not to mention the occasional escapist

Aaron Betsky (1958) has been the director of the Netherlands Architecture Institute in Rotterdam since 2001, and the author of among other things False Flat: Why Dutch Design Is so Good (Phaidon). He is currently working on a book on Modernism in architecture and general design. The damage done by hurricane Katrina in New Orleans has raised an acute problem which is addressed in the NAI exhibition Newer Orleans. What function can architecture and planning have after an event as disastrous and traumatic as this hurricane? Is it possible for small architectural and planning interventions to contribute influentially not only to the reconstruction process, but also to a more equitable urban society? Is there such a thing as a multiplier effect of architecture?

fantasy for those who can afford it). But now, with the rebuilding of an entire city on the line, don't we need at least to ask whether architecture can do more?

In New Orleans the greatest immediate need would seem to be for housing. Yet the provision of adequate dwellings for the displaced is not an activity in which architecture can play a role beyond making sure those houses are safe and sound and more or less aesthetically pleasing. Where the housing will be, how much of it there will be, how much it is likely to cost, and who will live there is currently being decided by politicians and, no doubt, real-estate interests. Architects are assisting in the design of new housing, but no one seems to be asking why anybody would return to New Orleans in the first place, let alone what they would do once they came back. The question "What will the new New Orleans be?" is hardly an idle one. Nowadays cities around the world are engaged in ruthless competition: every urban area needs its "unique selling points," and when a city builds infrastructure it does so not just to improve the lives of its inhabitants but also to attract investment. New Orleans had been losing this battle for quite some time. After a period of growth as the service hub for the Gulf Coast oil industry, it began ceding energy-sector and shipping jobs to Houston and other cities in the region long before Katrina brought the city's economic life to a standstill. The only revenue producer New Orleans had managed to maintain was tourism, but it struggled to expand that industry's base beyond the lure of the French Quarter's mythic libertine attractions. Old New Orleans was in decline. Katrina turned that gradual – and, to those who never ventured into the poorer wards, elegant – decay into catastrophe. Why would anyone come back?

New Orleans is now clearly, in all likelihood irrevocably, one of the world's "shrinking cities" – large metropolitan areas that emerged in earlier stages of industrialization and have now lost their economic base and a significant portion of their population. Detroit, Cleveland, and Buffalo are prominent examples in the United States, the Ruhr Valley the best-known European instance. What is interesting is the fact that nature is coming back in many of these areas – by default in the US and by design in Europe. The vast voids left by deindustrialization and depopulation are turning back into forest and field. In Germany, old ironworks are being converted into beautifully landscaped parks, such as the one in Duisburg-Nord (1999). As these shrinking cities nevertheless continue to sprawl into the far suburbs, turning more and more nature into miasmic built form, nature is returning into the inner city, and it can draw people back to these burned-out cores. At the same time, old cities still retain the legacy of their past achievements, in the forms of museums, concert halls, movie palaces, universities, libraries, historic mansions, and other cultural attractors that cannot easily be moved. Finally, old city neighborhoods that have held on to their historical character become attractive again because of their density and their propinquity to cultural amenities. And herein lie the elements for the rebirth of cities: new nature, old culture, and strong communities. We believe that these elements can also help

fig. 8.1   Plan Otto Wagner, Vienna

Erasmus Bridge, UN Studio   fig. 8.2
photo : UN Studio

New Orleans transform itself into a successful Newer Orleans – a smaller, more compact, and more beautiful city that would use its natural setting and cultural heritage to enhance viable neighborhoods and attract both new businesses and residents. To test this hypothesis and to provide concrete instances of what such a Newer Orleans might look like, we asked six architecture firms to consider these three core elements. We asked one Dutch and one American firm each to address the issues of how architecture could facilitate community, create an urban icon to house the city's cultural patrimony, and provide a way of connecting the city back to its landscape.

The decision to make this a Dutch-American effort was in part pragmatic, as the Netherlands Architecture Institute and the Dutch Ministries of Housing, Spatial Planning, and the Environment (VROM), Economic Affairs (EZ), and Transport, Public Works, and Water Management (V&W) supported the project. But at the same time we recognized that, in the past few decades, Dutch architecture has developed a conceptual approach to building that might be appropriate to the rethinking of New Orleans. The Dutch have become very good at seeing architecture not as the production of autonomous objects but as the gathering of information about a site, the reconsideration of forms from the past, and the application of technologies from other fields. These designers then synthesize the results of this amassing of material without direct reference to the immediate surroundings or surface issues like client programs. Instead, they use "deep planning" methods to understand the underlying issues at hand and in the end produce forms that articulate new structures of coherence. Thus Rem Koolhaas (the best-known proponent of this manner of working) can rethink the very idea of a library and produce the crystalline Seattle

fig. 8.3 Public Library 42nd street, New York
photo: unknown

Public Library (2004). Furthermore, half of the Netherlands lies no more than a few feet above sea level – and significant portions lie below it. Dutch architects and engineers – who, after all, built the most complex system of dikes, levees, canals, and pumping stations in the world – are, then, well attuned to the difficulties New Orleans faces at a time when global climate change is raising sea levels and making weather patterns less predictable.

American architects, on the other hand, are particularly good at producing strong forms. They know how to make iconic structures, from skyscrapers to mansions that stand tall and proud, showing off the wealth and skill that went into producing them. At their best, American architects can call up a legacy of craft and inventiveness to produce forms that amaze us with their beauty and interior spaces that awe us. And they do this while proclaiming the importance of the new and yet respecting the old. Frank Gehry may look as if he is producing forms out of nothing, but he is able to do this only because he is a master at controlling site, scale, material, and space.

These are, of course, broad generalizations, but they nevertheless describe general tendencies that have arisen from particular cultural traditions and economic realities. We sought to draw on the strengths of each to come up with new forms for New Orleans, on three different scales. On a local level, we asked two architects to design a new community focus for an impoverished ward separated from the Superdome (still under renovation due to storm damage) by a highway. In this neighborhood, Katrina only completed the disintegration caused by poverty, neglect, the breakdown of social structures, and the impact of drug use. Here, as in most inner-city neighborhoods, schools are – ironically, given the widespread failure of urban American public schools – the only mechanisms by which inhabitants can hope to escape. When schools work, they are havens that can create possibilities in the constricted world in which they are situated. Schools are not just places of education; they are community halls, meal programs, health-care providers, counseling centers, and even shelters in times of disaster.

We solicited a proposal from MVRDV (Winy Maas, Nathalie de Vries, Jacob van Rijs), a Rotterdam firm with an international practice, which has distinguished itself through the design of compact, seemingly simple volumes that are extremely complex in their spatial configuration. At the same time, the architects are not afraid to break open those boxes, cantilevering living rooms out of apartment buildings and breaking up rows of houses to create a village of brightly colored pavilions rather than the more typical cookie-cutter suburban housing development.

fig. 8.4 Swiss Re
photo: Nigel Young/Foster and Partners

Beach House Sullivan's Island, Huff + Gooden   fig. 8.5
photo:Robert Starling

They have extended their formal investigations in theoretical treatises like their recent KM3: Excursions on Capacity (ACTAR, 2006), which begins with the premise that human and natural resources should be more rationally distributed. For the New Orleans project they responded to a child's drawing of a hill in the middle of the floodwaters by designing a stack of school and community spaces that would also be higher ground should the floods return. We also invited Huff + Gooden Architects, a young African-American firm based in Charleston, South Carolina, and New York (Ray Huff and Mario Gooden are the principals) to look at this project from their perspective. Huff + Gooden is only nine years old and does not have a great deal of built work to its name. However, the firm's imaginative schemes for a History and Science Museum in Charleston (design completed 1998) and the Degaussing Office Building (design completed 2001) show the versatility of the firm's work, which responds to a given setting with strong and memorable form. In a design for a house commissioned to replace one destroyed by Hurricane Hugo, Huff + Gooden combined traditional craft with abstract shapes to create a simple yet forceful object. The sleek and angular school buildings they put forward here would stand as a symbol of hope in a devastated neighborhood.

On a citywide scale – where the question becomes "How one can turn the metropolis's cultural legacy into a physical attractor?" – we proposed erecting a new "mediatheque," or multimedia library, for downtown New Orleans. Long before Katrina, Mayor C. Ray Nagin had been advocating for a new public library downtown, and we thought the disaster might be the impetus for this dream finally to come to fruition in a project that would integrate new technologies with the store-

fig. 8.6 Interior Library, MVRDV Spijkenisse
image: MVRDV

Exterior Library, MVRDV Spijkenisse   fig. 8.7
image: MVRDV

house of knowledge the city shelters. Such a public building at the core of New Orleans's downtown would argue for the importance of a shared identity – in a way that the anonymous office buildings and hotels currently there do not. The mediatheque would fulfill the role courthouses and city halls once did, while plugging the city's residents into larger networks of knowledge.

We turned first to Dutch architect Ben van Berkel. His firm, UN (United Network) Studio, has long been a proponent of "deep planning," and the firm's manner of working has been to begin by gathering large amounts of data and then to mold them, with the help of the computer, into iconic form. UN Studio is currently designing a new train station at Arnhem, the Netherlands, and the Mercedes-Benz

Museum in Stuttgart (2006). Van Berkel has become increasingly interested in the cultural implications of form, investigating how masses and volumes seemingly the product of mathematical formulas can have a deeper human resonance. For the mediatheque, UN Studios chose to reference age-old memorials and monuments, revitalizing them by deploying current technologies to create both a symbolic and an actual place for New Orleanians to access their culture. We also called on Thom Mayne and his Los Angeles–based studio, Morphosis. Winner of the 2005 Pritzker Prize, Mayne has long been known for expressive forms that seem to rise with a machine-like force from the ground to create jagged and jarring spatial enclosures. Yet his structures have always been shaped by an attempt to understand and open up existing urban conditions. The Diamond Ranch High School (1999) in Pomona, California, for instance, is an extrusion of its hillside into angled buildings that also stand as larger versions of the small tract homes huddled below the school. Mayne is trained as an urban designer as well as an architect, and his interests have lately returned to the question of how we can unfold the city itself into new forms. He had already been asked by a private developer to make a proposal for New Orleans and thus could use our mediatheque project as a way of testing his ideas for the city.

fig. 8.8 Leidsche Rijn Park, West 8
image: West 8

fig. 8.9 Chrissy Field
photo : Hargreaves

Chrissy Field fig. 8.10
photo : Hargreaves

Finally, at the scale of the delta landscape, we asked two designers trained as landscape architects to reconsider New Orleans's largest public open space, City Park. This popular spot for gathering, recreation, and culture was completely destroyed by Katrina, with most of its vegetation drowned or killed by salt water. We thought this might be a place where New Orleanians could not only come together but also come to a renewed knowledge of and relationship with the delta's landscape. The park is located adjacent to one of the city's major canals and connected to a larger system of green spaces that are or could be in turn connected with the infrastructure that allows human beings to inhabit a region that is, essentially, an enormous swamp.

Adriaan Geuze, of the Dutch landscape firm West 8, is a trained horticulturist but works as a landscape architect, urban designer, and artist. He has been at the forefront of the argument that design must be enlisted to address global warming. Living and working in the Netherlands — 70 percent of which would be inundated were a major flood to occur — he has proposed making a place for water and integrating it into planning, rather than trying to resist it with dams and dikes in a Sisyphean struggle against nature. His inventive landscape architecture and planning has combined disparate elements and forms to make us aware of the artificiality even of what we think of as nature, while reinvigorating the city with a sense of play. In rethinking City Park, Geuze drew on his experience with water in the landscape to create a park that is a miniature of the whole delta and includes a new river as well as a water memorial. Similarly, American landscape architect George Hargreaves has been a pioneer in bringing back a sense of the natural setting so often "buried" underneath urban pat-

fig. 8.11 Mercedes Benz Museum, UN Studio
photo: Christan Richters / UN Studio

Diamond Ranch School of San Francisco fig. 8.12
Federal Building, Morphosis
photo: Tim Hursley

terns. In San Jose, California, for example, he revealed the long-neglected Guadalupe River – the waterway that had once been the city's raison d'être but had become little more than a sewer and a flood risk – turning it into a linear park that reconnected this sprawling city's various neighborhoods and natural biotopes (1998). He employed a similar strategy for Crissy Field (2001), the park he designed at the base of San Francisco's Golden Gate Bridge and for the site of the Sydney Olympics (2000). Making us aware of where we are and building with nature to reconnect us to that site has been at the core of Hargreaves's work. This is precisely his firm's approach to City Park. Hargreaves Associates proposes using the rebuilding and improvement of New Orleans's water infrastructure as an organizational element for new public spaces.

We gave our six design teams one month to produce their ideas for a Newer Orleans. The results were not polished proposals or completed plans but as images and forms meant to trigger discussion and widen the scope of possibilities for New Orleans's resurrection. All six projects seek to reconnect the city's residents to one another, to their city, and to their landscape. They seek to house a sense of community, attract attention and activity, and make the landscape visible. They propose a shared space, both physical and mental, around which the city could organize itself in a meaningful manner. And in so doing, they not only suggest an architecture for a Newer Orleans but also point out potential ways for making all of us at home in an increasingly alien world.

Team 10 and the Historic City

SUZANNE MULDER

Essay 09

ARCHITECTURE BULLETIN N° 01 | 2006

The work of Team 10 — a group of architects from many different European countries who formed a vanguard in the 1950s and 1960s — is highly relevant. Many of the themes that occupied the members of Team 10 during their famous meetings in the period 1953 to 1981 are resurfacing in today's architectural discourse. One of those themes is the relation between history and modern architecture.

Suzanne Mulder (1959) is an architectural historian and runs an independent research bureau in Amsterdam. She has published several articles on the architecture and planning of the nineteenth and twentieth centuries. Mulder was the curator of a major exhibition on Team 10 (Team 10 - A Utopia of the Present) which was held in the NAi in 2005-2006 and is on tour in 2006 and 2006 to New Haven, Paris, Milan etc. She is surprised about the ongoing conversation on traditionalism in architecture, in particular at the lack of historical awareness among architects and their clients; in the not so distant past, after all, Team 10 demonstrated how tradition could be given a contemporary interpretation in an intelligent way.

A renewed interest in history is making its mark in architecture and urban planning. In the Netherlands, in particular, a form of architectural traditionalism is currently gaining popularity. Although Dutch architecture enjoys a progressive reputation, contemporary clients and architects are increasingly opting for traditional-style solutions. New urban expansion areas are looking more and more like traditional villages, and in some cases like medieval castles. Freshly built "historic" gables and street façades, with modern complexes hidden behind them, are invading the Netherlands' historic city centers. The contemporary traditionalism of today's architecture may perhaps be explained by advancing globalization, which affects day-to-day life and causes people to become increasingly estranged from their living environment. This promotes a longing for security and recognizability, resulting in an increasing demand for housing estates and buildings with an individual and supposedly historical identity.

The past also figures significantly in Dutch government policy towards spatial planning and the built environment.

For some years now, the "conservation and renewal" of landscape heritage has been touted as a fundamental concept in several policy documents, such as the Belvedere Memorandum of 1999. These documents call for increased efforts to incorporate environmental heritage aspects into new-construction projects, on the argument that a historical dimension will contribute to spatial quality.

Unfortunately, present ways of dealing with environmental heritage often go no farther than retro-architecture, to turning historic inner cities into museums, and to reproducing historic forms without contemporary meaning. Does the copying of old visual idioms and the creation of historicizing vcity scenes respond to the demands for (a) conservation and renewal, and (b) identity and recognizability? Or can we picture a way in which tradition and history could form a basis for genuine innovation?

In this context, it is interesting to reexamine the ideas of Team 10 with regard to the incorporation of history and tradition. Terms that crop up in the contemporary discourse — such as the role of history in architecture, the importance of historic cities, identity and recognizability — featured decades ago in the discussions of Team 10. Aldo van Eyck (1918-1999), Giancarlo de Carlo (1918-2005), Alison and Peter Smithson (1928-1993 and 1923-2003 respectively), George Candilis (1913-1995) and Shadrach Woods (1923-1973) were especially interested in the possibly advantageous role the traditional city could play in the progressive modernization of society.

Philosophy

Just as the present hankering after the past may be seen as a reaction to the pervasive influence of globalization, Team 10's interest in history and tradition responded to the abstract and technocratic modernism that prevailed just after the Second World War. The architects of Team 10, who had become acquainted within CIAM, sought solutions for what they saw as the increasing alienation of people from their living surroundings. They opposed the rational, functionalist modernism of the kind favored by CIAM, which had spread all over the world in the form of enormous urban extension schemes and monotonous high-rise apartment buildings. In the same way as people are now turning to historic examples in search of recognizability and familiarity, the architects of Team 10 ranked the historic city and the primitive village as opposites to the sterile, anonymous postwar suburbs.

fig. 9.1   Collegio del Colle campus and studenthousing (1962-1966) Urbino, Giancarlo de Carlo
photo : Archivio Progretti

idem   fig. 9.2

Inevitably there are not only similarities but also major differences between then and now. Today's traditionalism, which has its roots in the postmodernism of the seventies and eighties, is marked by a revival of the past and is a reaction against the modernist philosophy in which newness is everything. Team 10, too, as offshoot of the Modern movement, nurtured an interest in traditional architecture that was not so much a product of conservatism as of a passion for renewal coupled with sincere social commitment and a longing for a new world in which people could achieve self-fulfillment both individually and collectively. Team 10's interest in the historic city was a part of their quest for new architectural and planning approaches that would centralize the specific need of users and residents, while also doing justice to the complexity of modern society.

The architects of Team 10 studied historical and traditional cities in order to probe the relation between social and physical structures. In the 1950s, for example, Candilis and Woods analyzed building and living in the bidonvilles and traditional villages of North Africa, and in the historic cities of Western Europe. Alison and Peter Smithson, during the same period, were interested in every-

day street life in working-class districts of London, and in hamlets in the English countryside. Giancarlo de Carlo studied spontaneous architecture in rural Italian villages and researched the medieval cities of Central Italy. Aldo van Eyck was fascinated by the Dogon villages of Central Africa and traveled the whole world to study ethnic cultures.

Team 10's interest in the historical and social dimensions of architecture was paired with an intense concern for the specific context of each design task. In their first joint document, the Doorn Manifesto of 1954, the group argued for a place-related approach to modern architecture, as opposed to the context-free tabula rasa of Modernism. They saw a new task for architecture in the discovery of architectural solutions that matched the specific attributes of a location, instead of resorting to preconceived universal solutions. In this respect, Team 10 introduced a new, more complete view of the city and of designing into modern architecture.

The members of Team 10 developed the notion of architecture as an "unfolding art", in which the design emerges from the investigation and analysis of the specific brief in conjunction with the social, economic, land-

fig. 9.3 idem

idem fig. 9.4

scape and historical context. They opposed a merely formal or esthetic approach to architecture, and dismissed the idea of the "autonomy of form" propagated by postmodern architects in the seventies and eighties. Team 10's inclusive design approach was of considerable influence on the work of countless contemporary architects and urban designers (including OMA/Rem Koolhaas).

Designs

Team 10 was not so much interested in recycling historic or traditional forms as in taking forward those structures and patterns that had developed through history. They always viewed those historical structures from a modern perspective. What mattered, as De Carlo put it, was taking trouble to "read" the historical context, "identifying the signs of physical space, extracting them from its stratifications, interpreting them and recomposing them in systems that will be significant for us today". Team 10 wished to show that traditional patterns of building and dwelling possessed a sustainability that made them transplantable to the modern urban context, where they could serve as solutions to contemporary problems.

How did Team 10 apply these ideas in their designs? The members developed several dif-

ferent urban planning models for mass housing which referred to elements of the historic city. Candilis-Josic-Woods devised the stem concept, in which a continuous pedestrian "street" with public facilities formed both the physical and the social backbone of the community. The group used this concept in, for example, their design for a large urban extension to Toulouse, the Toulouse-le-Mirail district (1962). The quality of the traditional city street as an important ingredient of the social fabric also underlay the street-in-the-air concept of Alison and Peter Smithson. This idea was eventually realized in the Robin Hood Gardens housing estate in London (1971). These structures were all intended to harmonize with the existing landscape or local context.

Buildings as City Fabric

Other hallmarks of the historic city which inspired the architects of Team 10 and which they used in their designs were the continuity and interweaving of private and public space, and the potential for varied use. They saw the model of the historically developed city as a viable alternative to the modernist notion of the functional city based on the separation of functions. In 1968 the Smithsons and Candilis-Josic-Woods designs are flexible structures with a capacity to accommodate

fig. 9.5 Lecture Hall 'il Magistrero' (1968–1976)
Urbino, Giancarlo de Carlo
photo : Archivio Progretti

Aerial-photo of Urbino from the south, fig. 9.6
with on the right 'il Magistero'

the accelerating growth and change of modern urban programs. These designs started with an analysis of the traditional fabric of European cities. The "web" concept, which Woods developed in 1962 and used in such projects as his building for the Free University of Berlin (1965), was a model that involved a minimal "fabric" within which a city or a building could develop flexibly, and which could accommodate various forms of appropriation and usage. The Smithsons developed the related concept of the "mat building", a term which emphasized the connectedness of buildings. Mat building was at a scale between those of architecture and urban planning, and was to serve as an infrastructure for buildings without fixing the functional program or form in advance. The Smithsons applied the idea in their competition entry for the future development of Kuwait City (1968, not realized).

Aldo van Eyck declared the principle of "a city like a house, and a house like a city". It was part of the configurative design method he applied to all his work. Underlying this design method was a reciprocal relation between the part and the whole, with a non-hierarchical, polycentric organization linking the different scales of the built environment. He drew his inspiration for it from an analysis of eth-

nic patterns of building and living in Africa. A widely known example of his architecture is the Municipal Orphanage in Amsterdam (1955-1960): a children's home conceived as a miniature city, with corridors like winding streets and successive pavilions like houses.

Giancarlo de Carlo too saw buildings as "little cities", as systems of spatial and social links. The Collegio del Colle (1962-1964), a student village in Urbino, illustrates this outlook. The university complex was designed as a network of connections and transitions between public, semi-public and private spaces. De Carlo found points of connection for this approach in the medieval town of Urbino, which like his modern complex gives the appearance of being a natural outgrowth of the hilly countryside. The central campus building is poised at the top of the hill, from where paths ramify in a seemingly random pattern to the individual student apartments. The building materials and the form language are explicitly modern and contemporary. The complex is a splendid example of De Carlo's subtle contextual approach, and testifies to his capacity to combine tradition with modernity. The real qualities of this project are not obvious until you see it in real life. Only then does it become clear that the human dimension and human perception form the basis of the

fig. 9.7   University Building 'il Magistero' Urbino
photo : Archivio Progretti

The Economist Building 1964,   fig. 9.8
Alison en Peter Smithson, London
photo: Avery Library NY

design, and that this can be achieved without any resort to -trite, dated or historizing architecture.

High Points: Inner City Projects

Team 10's outlook on the relation between history and modernity are best illustrated by a number of relatively small-scaled newconstruction projects in historic inner cities. The designs that relate in a real way to the historic urban context do most justice to the ideas of the Team 10 architects.

An early and still relevant example of a modern building in a historic inner city is The Economist building by Alison and Peter Smithson (London, 1959-1964). The design, which combines considerable subtlety in relation to the context with a radically modern approach, may be understood as a fragment of their much-discussed but unrealized design for Berlin Haupstadt (1958). In the Berlin scheme, the architects extended a huge, elevated pedestrian deck over the old city. The most striking aspect of the London design is the way the Smithsons integrated the headquarters of a modern company into the historical context of London's West End. The office complex consists of three separate towers of different heights forming an ensemble on an elevated plaza. Beneath the plaza, which

is reserved for pedestrians, there is a parking garage. The plinth follows the old building lines and encloses various public functions. The small tower's scale and placing relative to the building line conforms entirely to the historic buildings in the street. The largest tower is set back and its visual presence thus minimized. The plaza functions as an "in-between space" that mediates between the historic city and the new buildings. The architecture and the building materials are modern, yet the structure and dimensioning of the towers is such that they blend in with the existing urban fabric.

In the same period, Candilis-Josic-Woods created a design for the inner city Frankfurt, Frankfurt-Römerburg (1963). The idea of a web was literally applied into the urban structure in relation to the urban surroundings. The model photographs clearly demonstrate the potential of the web idea and show how the architects interwove their contemporary interpretation of historical structures with the existing fabric. The project was not realized, however, so it is impossible to judge whether this spectacular scheme would have stood the test of time.

The ideas of Aldo van Eyck similarly work best in inner city projects, in which he was

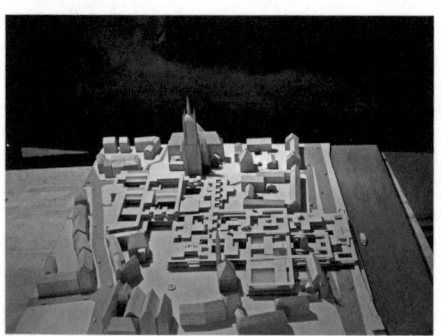 

fig. 9.9 Frankfurt-Römerberg, design for a new city
centre by Candilis-Josic-Woods, photo of
scale model, 1963
photo: Avery Library NY

idem fig. 9.10

required to insert newbuild into the existing urban fabric. His design for the city hall of Deventer (1966) demonstrates both his solicitous approach to the existing urban structure and buildings, and his modern contribution based on the configurative design method. The building is not treated as an autonomous entity but as a cluster of differentiated units which are embedded in the existing pattern of lots and alleys. The Deventer City Hall design forms structural bonds with the historic city in several ways: through its plastic form, through the spaces and through the routing. Yet this design is still considered a progressive example of modern building in a historic context. At the same time, for reasons including of the building materials used, it stands up as a contemporary work of architecture. This design was followed a few years later by another of Van Eyck's inner city projects, in this case built: the Hubertushuis, Amsterdam, (1973-1981), a shelter for single mothers and their children. Like Deventer City Hall, the building does not consist of a single, homogenous unit but of a complex of different components, reflecting the diversity of the historic urban context in which it is embedded.

The final example of a successful inner city project by members of Team 10 is "Il Magistero", a new university faculty building in the historic center of Urbino (1968-1974) by De Carlo. Here we encounter the same complex geometries and surprising glimpses between volumes. The building is one of many modern projects the architect realized in Urbino. In the Il Magistero building, De Carlo ingeniously combined a substantial program of functions, including lecture halls, a library, a cinema and a bar, all within the enclosing walls of an old monastery. He transformed the historic building into a highly modern six-storey complex without impairing the medieval city morphology. The new structures are practically invisible from the street, but they are clearly visible as one approaches the city from a distance, with the huge conical roof as the most prominent component. This project, too, exemplifies a respect for the human dimension free of triteness, the use of complex internal geometries and harmony between historic and modern forms.

Continuum

The architecture of Team 10 resists categorization. The individual architects posed themselves the same questions but came up with very different answers. De Carlo's projects in Urbino, the Smithsons' Economist building in London and Van Eyck's Hubertushuis in Amsterdam bear hardly any superficial resemblance to one another. They demonstrate however that members of Team 10 were responsible for some highlights of twentieth-century architecture in which history and modernity are equally respected, and in which elements of the traditional city were adopted, transformed and given contemporary meaning. These buildings are relevant answers to the question of how the past can be utilized as a basis for progressive architecture, and they can serve as useful examples in the present discussion on conservation and renewal. In these works by Team 10 members, the conventional polarization between the traditional and the modern seems to have been reconciled, and, in Van Eyck's words, "past, present and future are active as a continuum". Another of Van Eyck's statements is perhaps also worth quoting: "This is no concession to the past, not even a limited one. It's not a question of retreat, but one of awareness of what 'exists' in the present — of what has been carried forward into it: the projection of the past into the future via the realized present."

REFERENCES
- Archined. "Koolhaas of Krier? Discussie over het nieuwe traditionalisme", 2005 (www.archined.nl/archined/4970.0.html)
- Brons, R., Rodermond, J. and Wallagh, G. (eds.) Een cultuur van ruimte maken. Ontwerpen aan geschiedenis, Stimuleringsfonds voor Architectuur, Rotterdam, 2005
- Ligtelijn, V. (ed.), Aldo Van Eyck, Bussum, 1999
- Rodermond, J. (ed.), Ontwerpen aan geschiedenis
- Risselada, M. and Heuvel, D. Van den (eds.), Team 10 1953-1981. In Search of a Utopia of the Present, Rotterdam, 2005
- Mulder, S. (ed.), Team 10: A Utopia of the Present, NAI exhibition, 2005